The Pennsylvania
Old Assyrian Texts

HEBREW UNION COLLEGE ANNUAL SUPPLEMENTS

NUMBER 3

The Pennsylvania Old Assyrian Texts

W. C. Gwaltney Jr.

CINCINNATI, 1983

Published with the assistance of
The Neumann Memorial Publication Fund
established by Sidney Neumann as a memorial to his parents,
Abraham and Emma Neumann
and the
Henry Englander—Eli Mayer Publication Fund
established in their honor by
Esther Straus Englander and Jessie Straus Mayer

This paperback edition, 2015.

ISBN 13: 978-0-8229-6374-5
ISBN 10: 0-8229-6374-4

Typeset in the United States of America by
Eisenbrauns

Table of Contents

INTRODUCTION

The 82 tablets and fragments that constitute the unpublished Old Assyrian collection of the University Museum of the University of Pennsylvania are here offered in transliteration and translation, together with notes and indices. Line drawings are not included since Hildegard Lewy's were published posthumously in HUCA 39 (1968) pp. 1–33 and 40/41 (1969/70) pp. 45–85 with a few introductory remarks by S. N. Kramer. These texts had been read in 1956 by her husband Julius Lewy, who made transcriptions of them. Mrs. Lewy returned to Philadelphia in 1967 to collate them and to compare her readings with those of Benno Landsberger, whose notes remain with the texts. She had planned to prepare a critical edition of these unpublished texts, but ill health, culminating in her death three months after her visit, prevented her producing even preliminary translations or indices. She had scribbled a few notes in the margins of the rough transcription and collation sheets and had typed a three-page general comment entitled "Some of the outstanding features of the collection of Old Assyrian texts in the University Museum."

The present edition is based upon all the above-mentioned materials as well as a collation that I made in March 1976. I was unable to restudy Pa. 1 (=L 29–553, Tablet and Case) because it was on display at that time. Fortunately Julius Lewy had made this text a matter of detailed study in 1957. George Dales and S. N. Kramer had supplied him with several photographs and had collated several passages for him. Professor Lewy's notes and the photographs have provided me with the necessary help in translating Pa. 1.

Nearly 20,000 clay tablets have been excavated from Kültepe in central Turkey, the site of ancient Kanish. Of these, about 3,000 have appeared in line drawing. Of the 3,000, only about 800 or so have been published in translation, a mere 4% of the 20,000. Modern philological studies dealing with these Old Assyrian business documents are outstanding; but a significant step is being skipped—the publishing of texts in translation for a wider range of scholars to study. Furthermore, cuneiformists might consider collaborating with specialists in other disciplines on these texts. In the case of the Kültepe corpus, an economist might well work with a cuneiformist to produce an enlightening economic analysis of the Old Assyrian trade system.

With the addition in 1968 of Hecker's *Grammatik der Kültepe Texte* (= *Analecta Orientalia* 44) to the older works, we have sufficient tools to carry forward the all-important work of translation. Other excellent studies have brought greater precision to the present knowledge of the technical vocabulary of the "Cappadocian" tablets: Veenhof's *Aspects of Old Assyrian Trade and Its Terminology* (1972), Larsen's *Old Assyrian Caravan Procedures* (1967) and *The Old Assyrian City-State and Its Colonies* (1976), Hirsch's *Untersuchungen zur altassyrischen Religion* (1961), Orlin's *Assyrian Colonies in Cappadocia* (1970; see M. T. Larsen's review in JAOS 94 [1974] 468–475), and Garelli's *Les assyriens en Cappadoce* (1963). There will always be lacunae, misunderstood words and concepts, and missed nuances. The usual procedures of critical evaluation must continue to make translations more precise. But the larger percentage of renderings would be usable by a broader range of scholars. I offer this volume in the hope of providing more translated documentation for the exciting Old Assyrian period of expanded economic involvement in distant lands.

I have not used quotation marks in the texts to indicate the opening and closing of direct address since the extent of the direct address is often debatable.

I hope that the translations will not only reflect the scribes' thought but that they will also be readable to those not versed in the Old Assyrian dialect. Unfortunately, a few terms still stubbornly defy the scholars' best attempts at definition. The term *ḫamushtum*, designating a unit of days, is a good example. Explanations of its meaning have ranged from 5 to 50 days. One translator tried "week" as its meaning, which would lead the uninitiated astray, since no scholar has ever proposed 7 days for *ḫamushtum*. In this case and in similar cases, I have transliterated the term and hyphenated it with an English word that describes its category; for example, *ḫamushtum*-period or *pirikannū*-textiles.

I wish to acknowledge the help and encouragement of Dr. Samuel Greengus, curator of the Lewy collection at Hebrew Union College-Jewish Institute of Religion (Cincinnati), as well as Dr. David Weisberg and Dr. Matitiahu Tsevat, both of the faculty of Hebrew Union College-Jewish Institute of Religion in Cincinnati. Dr. Åke Sjöberg, curator of the Babylonian Section of the University Museum, University of Pennsylvania, and Dr. Erle Leichty, associate curator, were extremely kind and helpful in making the Pennsylvania Old Assyrian texts available during the rush of hosting the 1976 meeting of the American Oriental Society. Director John A. Brinkman and editor-in-charge of the *Chicago Assyrian Dictionary*, Erica Reiner, as well as the entire staff of the Oriental Institute of the University of Chicago, were most hospitable in opening the copious files of the CAD to me and providing the use of the full range of the Institute's facilities. Professor I. J. Gelb was also very kind and encouraging. The National Endowment for the Humanities is due a word of thanks for providing me a grant to study at the Oriental Institute in Professor Brinkman's Summer Seminar (1975) on Assyrian History. Milligan College's program of sabbatical leaves made it possible for me to be away from the classroom for the 1975-76 academic year to devote my full energies to this work of research and writing. Finally, I must acknowledge my debt to my teachers in the sometimes perilous ways of Old Assyrian, Julius and Hildegard Lewy, and especially to Mrs. Lewy who continued to offer instruction and advice above and beyond the call of duty even after I had completed my doctoral studies and left the Cincinnati area.

Milligan College, Tennessee
September 1981

ABBREVIATIONS AND SYMBOLS

The abbreviations used are for the most part those utilized in the *Chicago Assyrian Dictionary* and W. von Soden's *Akkadisches Handwörterbuch*. In addition the following abbreviations occur:

Dergi	= *Türk Tarih, Arkeologya ve Etnografya Dergisi*
Gelb	= I. J. Gelb, *Inscriptions from Alishar and Vicinity* (OIP 27)
Hirsch UAR or UAR	= H. Hirsch, *Untersuchungen zur altassyrischen Religion* (AfO Beiheft 13/14)
Pa.	= University of Pennsylvania Museum Old Assyrian Texts

The following diacritical signs are fully applied in the transliterations but only sparingly in the translations.

[ ]	wholly lost
[[ ]]	erased
⌜ ⌝	partially lost
< >	omitted by the scribe
≪ ≫	pleonastically written by the scribe
( )	supplied by the author
*	reconstructed form
/	alternative reading
<	develops out of
>	develops into
!	sign abnormal in form, but must be read as transliterated
x	a single lost or unreadable sign
. . .	lost or unreadable signs, number uncertain or unessential

TEXTS, TRANSLATIONS AND NOTES

Pa. 1 A = L 29-553 Inner Tablet

1. DU$_{10}$-*ṣí-lá-A-šùr* DUMU *Bu-zi-a*
2. *E-me-nu-um* DUMU *Ás-qú-dim*
3. *i-na mì-ig-ra-tí-šu-nu*
4. *iṣ-bu-tù-ni-a-tí-ma ni-iš*
5. *a-lim*^{ki} *it-mu lu*$^{!}$ *i-ta-ma E-me-nu-um*
6. *i-na ší-ga-ri-im*
7. *ša A-šùr* 3 GÍN KÙ.BABBAR
8. *i-na ḫa-ra-ni-im*
9. *a-na ba-ri-šu-nu*
10. *E-me-nu-um lu ig-mu-ru-ni*
11. *a-na* 2/3 GÍN KÙ.BABBAR

Edge 12. *sà-ḫa-ar-tá-šu*

13. DU$_{10}$-*ṣí-lá-A-šùr*

Rev. 14. *a-na E-me-ni-im*

15. *lu i-dí-ú-šu-ni*
16. *tap-pá-ú-tám lá e-pu-šu-ni*
17. 2 GÍN KÙ.BABBAR DU$_{10}$-*ṣí-lá-A-šùr*
18. *a-na ba-ri-šu-nu lá ig-mu-ru*
19. *i-ta-ma-ma* 2 1/6 GÍN KÙ.BABBAR
20. DU$_{10}$-*ṣí-lá-A-šùr a-na*
21. *E-me-ni-im i-ša-qal*
22. 1 1/2 GÍN KÙ.BABBAR *ša a-na kà-ú-nim*
23. *E-me-nu-um ša a-na*
24. DU$_{10}$-*ṣí-lá-A-šùr i-dí-nu*

Edge 25. *ba-lúm ma-mì-tim i-ša-qal*

26. *E-na-A-šùr* DUMU *Puzúr-A-na*
27. *A-šùr-na-ṣí-ir*

Left Edge 28. DUMU *A-aḫ-Ištar A-šùr-li-bi-i* DUMU *Ba-ba-li*

29. *a-wi-lu a-ni-ú-tum*$_8$ *da-a-a-nu*

Pa. 1 B = L 29–553 Case

1. KIŠIB *E-na-A-šùr*$^{!}$ DUMU [*Puzúr-A-*]*na*
2. KIŠIB *A-šùr-na-ṣí-ir* DUMU *A-aḫ-Ištar*
3. KIŠIB *A-šùr-li-bi-i* DUMU *Ba-bi-lim*
4. DU$_{10}$-*ṣi-*≪DU$_{10}$-≫*lá-A-šùr* DUMU *Bu-zi-a*
5. *ú E-me-num* DUMU *Ás-qú-dim i-na mì-ig*$^{!}$*-ra-tí-šu-nu*
6. *iṣ-ba-at-ni-a-tí-ma ni-iš a-lim*^{ki}
7. *it-mu-ú-ma i-ta-ma E-me-nu-um*
8. *i-na ší-ga-ri-im ša A-šùr*
9. 3 GÍN KÙ.BABBAR *E-me-nu-um*
10. *i-na ḫa-ra-nim a-ba-ri-šu-nu*
11. *lu ig*$^{!}$*-mu-ru-ni a-na* 2/3 GÍN

Rev. 12. KÙ.BABBAR *sà-ḫa-ar-tá-šu* DU$_{10}$-*ṣí-lá-A-šùr*
13. *a-na E-me-ni-im lu i-dí-nu-ni*
14. 2 GÍN KÙ.BABBAR DU$_{10}$-*ṣí-lá-A-šùr*
15. *a-na ba-ri-šu-nu lá ig-mu-ru-ni*
16. *tap-pá-ú-tám lá e-pu-šu-ni*
17. *i-ta-ma-ma* 2 1/6 GÍN KÙ.BABBAR
18. DU$_{10}$-*ṣí-lá-A-šùr a-na E-me-ni-im*
19. *i-ša*$^{!}$*-qal* 1 1/2 GÍN KÙ.BABBAR
20. *ša E-me-nu-um a-na* DU$_{10}$-*ṣí-lá-A-šùr*
21. *a-na kà*$^{!}$*-ú-nim i-dí-nu-šu-ni*
22. *ba-lúm ma-mì-tim* KÙ.BABBAR
23. *i-ša-qal-šu-um*

Translation of Pa. 1 A = L 29–553 Tablet

(1) Ṭāb-ṣilla-Asshur son of Buzia (and) (2) Emenum son of Asqudum (3) on their initiative (4) called our court into session (lit., seized us) and swore the oath (5) of the City (of Assur). He swore (to the following statement): When Emenum (10) in truth completely paid (7) 3 shekels of silver (8) from the caravan profits (6) in the "door band" (7) of Asshur (9) on behalf of both of them; (and) when (13) Ṭāb-ṣilla-Asshur (15) deposited (12) his stock(14) for Emenum (11) for 2/3 of a shekel of silver; (and) (16) when they did not form a partnership; (18) (and) when (17) Ṭāb-ṣilla-Asshur (18) did not pay off (17) the 2 shekels of silver (18) for both of them, (19) he took an oath (that) (21) Ṭāb-ṣilla-Asshur will weigh out (19) 2 1/6 shekels of silver (20) to (21) Emenum. (25) He will (further) weigh out without an oath (22) the

1 1/2 shekels of silver which (23) Emenum (24) gave (23) to (24) Ṭāb-ṣilla-Asshur (22) for "confirming." (26) Enna-Asshur son of Puzur-Ana, (27) Asshur-nāṣir (28) son of Aḫ-Ishtar, (and) Asshur-libbī son of Bābā-(i)lī—(29) these gentlemen (are) the judges.

Translation of Pa. 1 B = L 29–553 Case

(1) The seal of Enna-Asshur son of [Puzur-A]na, (2) the seal of Asshur-nāṣir son of Aḫ-Ishtar, (3) the seal of Asshur-libbī son of Bāb(ā)-ilum. (4) Ṭāb-ṣilla-Asshur son of Buzia (5) and Emenum son of Asqudum on their initiative (6) called our court into session (lit., seized us) and (7) swore (6) the oath of the City (of Assur). (7) He swore (to the following statement): when (9) Emenum (11) in truth paid (9) 3 shekels of silver (8) in the "door band" of Asshur (10) for both of them from the caravan profits (and) when (12) Ṭāb-ṣilla-Asshur (13) gave (12) his stock (13) to Emenum (11) for 2/3 of a shekel (12) of silver (and) when (14) Ṭāb-ṣilla-Asshur (15) did not pay off (14) the 2 shekels of silver (15) for the both of them (and) when (16) they did not form a partnership, (17) he took an oath (that) (18) Ṭāb-ṣilla-Asshur (19) will weigh out (17) 2 1/6 shekels of silver (18) to Emenum. (23) He will (further) weigh out (22) without an oath (19) 1 1/2 shekels of silver (20) which Emenum (21) had given (20) to Ṭāb-ṣilla-Asshur (21) for "confirming."

Notes on Pa. 1 A = L 29–553 Tablet

Line 1— The conjunction *u* is expected at the end of the line but is definitely missing as shown by several collations since 1956. Notice that the conjunction is also missing in line 28.

Lines 2 and following— The PN Emenum is unknown to me elsewhere. Asqudum is attested, though not frequently.

Line 3— *Ina migrātišunu* is from *migrum*, "consent, agreement," see AHw 651a. See also J. Lewy RA 35 (1938) 88, where he translated Driver AnOr 6 (1933) pl. 4b:11.

Line 5— A photo of our text shows this line as being very squeezed. The remains favor *lu* over *ú*.

Line 6— *Šigarum* probably designates a place or chamber in the Asshur Temple since *ina* is used with it rather than *maḫar*. See AHw 1231a.

Line 10— Note the repetition of the PN Emenum as the subject of the verb. See also line 9 of the Case.

Line 15— Note that line 15 of the Tablet has *iddi'ūšūni* from *nadā'um*, "to deposit," while the Case (line 13) has *iddinūni* from *nadānum*, "to give."

Line 22— The translation of this infinitive remains a crux. See CAD K 170b, sub 3′. Earlier H. Lewy privately suggested "to alloy" but later rendered it "to invest."

Line 28— For the PN Bābā-ilī/um, "Bābā is (my) god", see Hirsch UAR 31f. and EL I 190, n.a. See also *Ba-ba-lá* in TuM 1, 2a:x + 5; Chantre 13:4′; CCT 5, 9b: 1, 3, 11; and TC 1, 68:4 (son of *Pe-ru-a*), 7 (ib.) and *Ba-ba-là-a* in Chantre 2:6.

Note on Pa. 1 B = L 29–553 Case

Line 1— The patronymy of Enna-Asshur is to be restored in the lacuna by referring to line 26 of the Inner Tablet.

Pa. 2 = L 29–555

1. 10 MA.NA KÙ.BABBAR *ṣa-ru-pá-am*
2. *A-šùr-na-da a-na ša-na-at*
3. *a-na I-dí-Ištar i-da-an-ma*
4. *a-ṣé-er* 10 MA.NA KÙ.BABBAR
5. *ni-[is-]ḫa-tim ú ša-du-a-tám*
6. *I-dí-Ištar i-na-dí-ma*
7. *i-re-eš*$_{15}$ KÙ.BABBAR *ša A-šùr-na-da*
8. *a-na I-dí-Ištar i-du-nu*
9. *ṭup-pu-um ša* 29 MA.NA
10. *ša I-dí-Ištar i-lá-pá-at-ma*
11. KÙ.BABBAR *a-ni-um ší-ni-šu*
12. *a-na a-lim*^{ki} *i-lá-ak-ma*
13. 29 MA.NA KÙ.BABBAR-*áp-šu*

Edge 14. *A-šùr-na-da i-lá-qí-ma*

Rev. 15. *šu-ma* DIRIG[[ ]]

16. *I-dí-Ištar i-lá-qí šu-ma*
17. *ba-ti-iq I-dí-Ištar ú-ma-lá*
18. *iš-tù* ITI 1 KAM *Ma-ḫu-ur*-DINGIR
19. *li-mì-im ša* ⌜*qá-*⌝*tí I-ku-pí-Ištar*

20. *ṭup-pu ḫa-ru-mu-tum*
21. *lu ša Kà-ni-iš lu ša Dur*$_4$*-ḫu-mì-id*
22. *lu ša Ku-na-na-ma-at*
23. *lu ša Dan-A-šur* DUMU *Šál-me-ḫi-im*
24. *mì-ma ṭup-pí ḫa-ru-mu-tim*
25. *pá-ni-ú-tim ša ḫu-bu-ul*
26. *I-dí-Ištar a-ma-šu* IGI *I-ri-ší-im*
27. IGI ^{d}IM-*ṣú-lu-li*
28. IGI ⌜*Pí-*⌝*lá-aḫ-A-šur*

Translation of Pa. 2 = L 29–555

(2) Asshur-nādā (3) will give (1) 10 manas of refined silver (2) for a year (3) to Īdī-Ishtar and (6) Īdī-Ishtar will deposit (5) the import tax and the *šaddū'atum*-tax (4) on the 10 manas of silver; (6) and (7) from the available silver which Asshur-nādā (8) is giving to Īdī-Ishtar, (9) a tablet of (i.e., recording) the 29 manas (10) (owed by) Īdī-Ishtar is to be written; and (11) this silver (12) will come to the City (of Assur) (11) a second time, (12) and (14) Asshur-nādā will take possession of (13) his 29 manas of silver; (14) and (15) if there is any additional (silver), (16) Īdī-Ishtar will take (it). If (17) any (silver) is missing, Īdī-Ishtar will make up the difference. (18) From the month of Maḫḫur-ilī, (19) the eponymy of Ikū(n)-pī-Ishtar's successor. (20) As far as the sealed tablets are concerned—(21) whether of Kanish, of Durḫumid, (22) of Kunanamat, (23) whether of Dan-Asshur son of Shalme-aḫum—(26) I will remove (24) whatever (25) earlier (24) sealed tablets (there may be) (25) of (i.e., recording) the debt of (26) Īdī-Ishtar. In the presence of Irishum, (27) in the presence of Adad-ṣulūlī, (28) (and) in the presence of Pilaḫ-Asshur.

Notes on Pa. 2 = L 29–555

Line 5— For *nisḫatum*, "import tax," see Veenhof AOATT 85f., 137, 333, 370, 398f. For *šaddū'utum*, see Veenhof AOATT 278–288.

Line 6— *I-na-dí-ma* may be understood as *inaddin-ma* from *nadānum* or as *inaddi-ma* from *nadā'um*.

Line 8— *I-du-nu* derives from *iddanu* by vowel harmony.

Line 10— *I-lá-pá-at-ma* must be understood as an N form with *ṭuppum* of line 9 as the subject.

Line 22— *Ku-na-na-ma-at* as a GN usually appears as *Ku-na-na-mì-it*. See KTS 19a:19; BIN 6, 133:21$^!$; CCT 2, 23:37; CCT 3, 7a:21. The nisbe of the latter name appears in CCT 2, 23:11 and TC 3, 209:24.

Line 26— *A-ma-šu* from *mašā'um*, "to remove by force, rob" (see AHw 624f.), not *mašû*, "to forget" (see AHw 631f.).

Pa. 3 = L 29–556

1. *a-na A-šur-na-da qí-bi*$_4$*-ma*
2. *um-ma* LUGAL-^{d}IM-*ma*
3. 3$^?$ GÚ 10 MA.NA AN.NA *ku-nu-ki*
4. 3 ANŠE$^{\text{ḫi.a}}$ *ṣa-lá-mì ku-ta-ni*
5. *i-na wa-ṣa-i-a / ba-ab a-bu-lim*
6. *A-šur-i-dí / ip-qí-dam i-na*
7. *kà-ri-im / a-šar ni-ru-bu*
8. TÚG$^{\text{ḫi.a}}$ / *a-ša-lá-aḫ-ma*
9. *a-pá-qí-id-ma / mu-nu-sú-nu*
10. *a-ša-pá-ra-kam i-na*
11. *ma-aḫ-ri-a / ú-lá iš-ma*

Edge 12. *mu-nu-sú-nu / ú-lá i-dí*

Rev. 13. 2/3 MA.NA KÙ.BABBAR / *a-qá-tí-a*
14. *i-dí-nam / um-ma A-šur-i-dí-ma*
15. 17 MA.NA AN.NA
16. *i-mu-ta-tí-im / ša-ki-in*
17. *a-qá-tí-kà li-qí*
18. *a-ša-ar-ma*$^!$ / *za-ku-sà*
19. *a-ša-pá-ra-ku-um a-ḫi*
20. *a-ta ga-am-ru-um ma-ad*
21. *a-na A-ni-nim / šu-up-ra-ma*
22. *šu-uq-lá-an / lá i-pá-tí-a*
23. *ú-ul* KÙ.BABBAR / *šé-bi*$_4$*-lam*

Edge 24. *ṣí-pá-ra-tim ša* KÙ.BABBAR
25. 2 ⌜GÍN⌝ *šé-bi*$_4$*-lam*

Translation of Pa. 3 = L 29–556

(1) To Asshur-nādā speak! (2) Thus (says) Sharra-Adad: (6) Asshur-īdī entrusted to me (3) 3(?) talents (and) 10 manas of tin (bearing) seals

(4) (and) 3 black donkey loads of cloths (5) at (the time of) my departure (from) the town gate. (8) I will deduct the textiles (6) at (7) the Mercantile Center (i.e., the *kārum*) wherever we enter (8) and (9) I will entrust (them) and (10) I will send word to you (indicating) (9) their number. (10, 11) Before my (departure) he did not hear; (12) he did not know their number. (14) He gave (13) 2/3 of a mana of silver into my hand.

(14) Thus (says) Asshur-īdī: (15) 17 manas of tin (16) have been placed in a container; (17) take (it) into your control. (18) I will watch (over it) and (19) I will send word to you (18) (of) its condition. (20) You (are) (19) my brother. (20) The outlay is great! (21) Send word to Aninum that (lit., and) (22) the two packages should not be opened. (23) Send no silver. (25) (Rather) ship 2 shekels' (weight) (24) of silver utensils.

Notes on Pa. 3 = L 29–556

Line 2— Sharra-Adad is known from BIN 4, 189:9 and ICK 1, 60:21 (a witness).

Line 4— See Veenhof AOATT 89–95 and 145–151 for the latest discussion of *kutānum*. We shall consistently translate the singular of *kutānum* as "cloth" and the plural as "cloths."

Line 5— For *bāb abullim*, see CAD A_1 84a and Larsen, OACP 28 (citing Landsberger Dergi 4 [1940] 11, n. 1).

Line 8— For the rare root *šalāḫum*, "to pull out, tear away," see AHw 1142a.

On the translation of TÚG$^{\text{ḫi.a}}$ (*ṣubātū*) see AOATT, chapter five (pages 89–97) for Veenhof's argument that *ṣubātum* must be taken as "textiles," not "garments." We shall translate the singular of *ṣubātum* as "textile" and the plural, "textiles."

Line 9— See Larsen, OACP 26 f., where *paqādum* is shown to mean "to entrust" either for shipment or investment. On p. 93 he takes *paqādum* as "to hand over for further action." Thus it is likely that the "entrustment" meant in line 9 is an investment of the textiles for profit with an unnamed person.

Line 10— In *ašapparakam*, the *kam* seems to be a scribal mistake for *kum*. Note that the scribe spelled out the dative in line 19 as *ku-um*.

Lines 13 and 17— *Ana qātia/ka* may also be translated "into my/your account" or "as my/your share."

Line 16— Collation shows the correctness of the reading *i-mu-ta-tim ša-ki-in* as against Veenhof's rendering (AOATT 32), *i-mu-ta-tim ku-nu-ki-ni*.

For *muttatum*, plural *muttātum*, "container(s) of half a load," see J. Lewy, OrNS 15 (1946) 396, n. 5; H. Lewy, RSO 39 (1964) 182f. and 188, n. 2 as well as AHw 690a. H. Lewy (RSO 39 [1964] 188, n. 2) showed that the terms *muttatum* and *šuqlum* were synonymous.

Line 18— The fourth sign is *ma* by collation.

Line 22— The traces favor *lá i-pá-ṭí-a* as against Veenhof's reading (AOATT 17f.) *lá i-ma-ṭí-a*.

Šuqlān, "two packages," in the nominative case requires the following verb, *patā'um*, to be an N form rather than G. See AHw 861.

Line 24— For *ṣiparātum*, see J. Lewy, JAOS 78 (1958) 94, n. 33, "nail, claw, pointed," AHw 1097a, "a small household utensil," and CAD Ṣ 154. Veenhof offers no suggestion as to the meaning of *ṣiparātum* (AOATT 122, n. 202) except to read "s" instead of "ṣ." See below, text 76:2′.

Pa. 4 = L 29–557

1. 2 1/2 MA.NA KÙ.BABBAR *ṣa-ru-pá-am i-ṣé-er*
2. *A-šur-i-mì-tí* / DUMU *I-ku-pì-Ištar*
3. ^{d}*En-líl-ba-ni i-šu* / *iš-tù ḫa-muš-tim*
4. *ša En-na-nim* DUMU *Šu-Ḫu-bu-ur*
5. 1 GÍN TA *a-na* 1 MA.NA-*im i-na* ITI KAM
6. *ṣí-ib-tám ú-ṣa-áb* ITI KAM *Ku-zal-li*
7. *li-mu-um A*-gu_5-*tum*
8. 6 MA.NA KÙ.BABBAR *ṣa-ru-pá-am i-ṣé-er kà-ri-im*
9. ^{d}*En-líl-ba-ni i-šu iš-tù ḫa-muš-tim*
10. *ša Kur-ub-Ištar* ITI KAM *ša Sà-ra-tim li-mu-um*
11. *ša qá-tí En-na*-ZU.IN 2/3 GÍN 15 ŠE TA
12. *i-na* ITI KAM *a-na* MA.NA-*im ú-ṣú-bu*
13. 2 MA.NA KÙ.BABBAR *ṣa-ru-pá-am i-ṣé-er*
14. *A-šùr-mu-ta*-bi_4-il_5 DUMU *Pu-šu-ki-in*
15. ^{d}*En-líl-ba-ni i-šu iš-tù ḫa-muš-tim*
16. *ša En-nam-A-šur* DUMU *Šál-me-ḫi-im*
17. ITI KAM *Kán-mar-ta li*-<*mu-um*> *Ma-ṣí-ì-lí*
18. 1 GÍN TA *ṣí-ib-tám ú-ṣa-áb*
19. 2 1/3 MA.NA KÙ.BABBAR *ṣa-ru-pá-am i-na* / MA.NA-*i-a*

20. KÙ.BABBAR *wa-du i-*[*ṣé-er*] *Sú-ku-a* DUMU *A-šur-i-dí*

21. *En-líl-ba-*[*ni i-*]*šu* <*iš-tù*> *ḫa-muš-tim*

22. *ša Púzur-*[*Ištar*] ITI KAM *Kán-mar-ta*

23. *li-mu-um A-gu*$_5$*-tum* 1 GÍN TA

Edge 24. *ṣí-ib-tám ú-ṣa-áb*

25. 1 1/2 MA.NA KÙ.BABBAR *ṣa-ru-*<*pá-*>*am i-ṣé-er*

26. *A-lá-ḫi-im* DUMU *Šál-ma-A-šur*

27. *En-líl-ba-ni i-šu iš-tù*

28. *ḫa-muš-tim ša A-ḫu-qar* ITI KAM *Qá-ra-a-tim*

29. *li-mu-um Ma-ṣí-ì-lí* 1 GÍN TA

30. *ṣí-ib-tám ú-ṣa-áb* 1 MA.NA KÙ.BABBAR

31. *ṣa-ru-pá-am i-ṣé-er* ^{d}IM-GAL *ú Šu-*ZU.IN

32. DUMU *Puzúr-A-na* ^{d}*En-líl-ba-ni i-šu*

33. *iš-tù ḫa-muš-tim ša En-nam-A-šur*

34. 1 1/2 GÍN TA *ṣí-ib-tám ú-ṣú-bu* ITI KAM

35. *Kán-mar-ta li-mu-um Ma-ṣí-ì-lí*

36. 2 MA.NA KÙ.BABBAR *ṣa-ru-pá-am i-ṣé-er*

37. *Bu-za-zu* ^{d}*En-líl-ba-ni i-šu iš-tù*

38. *ḫa-muš-tim ša Lu-zi-na* ITI KAM

39. *Be-el-tí-*É.GAL*-lim li-mu-um ša qá-tí*

40. *A-gu*$_5$*-tim* 1 GÍN TA *i-na* ITI KAM

41. *ṣí-ib-tám ú-ṣa-áb*

42. 1 MA.NA 15 GÍN KÙ.BABBAR *ṣa-ru-pá-am*

43. *i-ṣé-er* / *A-šur-*GAL DUMU *Lá-qí-pì-im*

44. ^{d}*En-líl-ba-ni i-šu iš-tù ḫa-muš-tim*

45. *ša I-ku-pì-a* DUMU *Šu-A-nim li-mu-um*

46. *En-na-*ZU.IN ITI KAM / *A-lá-na-tim*

47. 1 1/2 GÍN TA *ṣí-ib-tám ú-ṣa-áb*

48. 1/2 MA.NA KÙ.BABBAR *ṣa-ru-pá-am i-ṣé-er*

49. DU$_{10}$*-ṣí-lá-A-šùr* DUMU *Puzúr-*^{d}MUŠ

Edge 50. ^{d}*En-líl-ba-ni i-šu iš-tù*

51. *ḫa-muš-tim ša I-dí-a-bi*$_4$*-im* ITI KAM

52. *Áb Ša-ra-ni*

Left Edge 53. *li-mu-um ša qá-tí A-gu*$_5$*-tim* 1 1/2 GÍN TA *ṣí-ib-tám ú-ṣa-áb*

54. 2/3 MA.NA KÙ.BABBAR *ṣa-ru-*<*pá-*>*am i-ṣé-er Puzúr-*^{d}UTU *ú A-šur-i-mì-tí me-er-ú*

55. *Šu-Nu-nu* ^{d}*En-líl-ba-ni i-šu iš-tù ḫa-muš-tim ša A-šur-iš-ta-ki-il*$_5$

56. ITI KAM *Tí-i-na-tim li-mu-um Ma-ṣí-ì-lí a-na* ITI KAM *i-ša-qú-lu*

57. ⌜*šu-*⌝*ma lá iš-qú-lu* 1 1/2 GÍN TA *a-na* 1 MA.NA-*im* *ṣí-ib-tám ú-ṣú-bu*

Translation of Pa. 4 = L 29–557

(3) Enlil-bāni has (1) a debt of 2 1/2 manas of refined silver against (2) Asshur-imittī son of Ikū(n)-pī-Ishtar. (3) (Dating) from the *ḫamushtum*-period (4) of Enna-Anum son of Shū-Ḫubur (6) he will pay interest at the rate of (5) 1 shekel per mana per month. (6) (Dated to): the month of Kuzalli, (7) the eponymy of Agutum.

(9) Enlil-bāni has (8) a debt of 6 manas of refined silver against the Mercantile Center (*kārum*). (9) (Dating) from the *ḫamushtum*-period (10) of Kurub-Ishtar, the month of Sarrātum, the eponymy (11) of Enna-Su'en's successor, (12) they will pay interest at the rate of (11) 2/3 of a shekel (and) 15 grains (12) per month per mana.

(15) Enlil-bāni has (13) a debt of 2 manas of refined silver against (14) Asshur-muttabbil son of Pūshu-kēn. (15) (Dating) from the *ḫamushtum*-period (16) of Ennam-Asshur son of Shalme-aḫum, (17) month of Kanwarta, eponymy of Maṣṣi-ilī, (18) he will add interest at the rate of 1 shekel per (mana per month).

(21) Enlil-bāni has (19) a debt of 2 1/3 manas of refined silver (20) verified (19) by my (20) silver (19) mana-weight (20) against Suku'a son of Asshur-īdī. (21) <(Dating) from> the *ḫamushtum*-period (22) of Puzur-Ishtar!, the month of Kanwarta, (23) the eponymy of Agutum, (24) he will pay interest at the rate of (23) 1 shekel per (mana per month).

(27) Enlil-bāni has (25) a debt of 1 1/2 manas of refined silver against (26) Āl(i)-aḫum son of Shalma-Asshur. (27) (Dating) from the *ḫamushtum*-period of Aḫu-waqar, the month of Qarrātum, (29) the eponymy of Maṣṣi-ilī, (30) he will pay interest at the rate of (29) 1 shekel per (mana per month).

(32) Enlil-bāni has (30) a debt of 1 mana of (31) refined (30) silver (31) against Adad-rabi and Shū-Su'en (32) son of Puzur-Ana. (33) (Dating) from the *ḫamushtum*-period of Ennam-Asshur, (34) they will pay interest at the rate of 1 1/2 shekels per (mana per month). (Dated to): the month of (35) Kanwarta, eponymy of Maṣṣi-ilī.

(37) Enlil-bāni has (36) a debt of 2 manas of refined silver against (37) Buzazu. (Dating) from (38) the *ḫamushtum*-period of Luzina, the month of (39) Bēlti-ekallim, the eponymy of (40) Agutum's (39) successor,

(41) he will pay interest at the rate of (40) 1 shekel (per mana) per month.

(44) Enlil-bāni has (42) a debt of 1 mana (and) 15 shekels of refined silver (43) against Asshur-rabi son of Lā-qēpum. (44) (Dating) from the *ḫamushtum*-period (45) of Ikū(n)-pīa son of Shū-Anum, the eponymy of (46) Enna-Su'en, the month of Allānātum, (47) he will pay interest at the rate of 1 1/2 shekels per (mana per month).

(50) Enlil-bāni has (48) a debt of 1/2 of a mana of refined silver against (49) Ṭāb-ṣilla-Asshur son of Puzur-Niraḫ. (50) (Dating) from (51) the *ḫamushtum*-period of Īdī-abum, the month of (52) Ab Sharrāni, (53) the eponymy of Agutum's successor, he will pay interest at the rate of 1 1/2 shekels per (mana per month).

(55) Enlil-bāni has (54) a debt of 2/3 of a mana of refined silver against Puzur-Shamash and Asshur-imittī sons of (55) Shū-Nunu. (Dating) from the *ḫamushtum*-period of Asshurish-takil, (56) the month of Ti'inātum, the eponymy of Maṣṣi-ilī, within a month they shall weigh out (the silver). (57) If they have not weighed out (the silver), they will add interest at the rate of 1 1/2 shekels per mana (per month).

Notes on Pa. 4 = L 29–557

Lines 3, 9, 15, 21, 28, 33, 38, 44, 51, and 55— The usual order of *ḫamuštum*, MN, and eponymy suggests that the *ḫamuštum*-period was shorter than a month, that is, the scribe noted the most specific time designation, then the next most specific, and finally the least specific. The slight alteration of this order in lines 44–46 seems to be the result of a scribal oversight. One wonders why the most specific time datum is curiously missing from the OA system of time reckoning, that is, the day of the month, or the day of the *ḫamuštum*.

Lines 10f., 39, and 53— For the expression *līmum ša qāti* PN, see Kienast, ATHE p. 4, note on text 1:15.

Lines 17, 22, and 35— For this reading of the MN, see V. Donbaz, JCS 24 (1972) 24–28.

Lines 19–21— The rendering of *ina* MA.NA-*i-a* KÙ.BABBAR *wa-du* is suggested by Veenhof (AOATT 58), who understands *waddū/uddū* as a D stative of *idā'um* in the sense of "to verify." See GKT Section 97d.

Lines 21f.— EL 44:7 (Jena 279) has the *ḫamuštum* of Puzur-Ishtar.

Line 34— The remains at the beginning of the line may be interpreted variously: 3, 2, 1 1/2, 5/6, 2/3, or 1/3. After collation 1 1/2 is clear.

Pa. 5 = L 29–558

1. *um-ma A-šùr-i-dí-ma / a-na*

2. *A-aḫ-Ištar A-la-ḫi-im Ì-lí-a-lim*

3. *ù A-šùr-ta-ak-lá-ku*

4. *qí-bi$_4$-ma* 2 GÚ 1 MA.NA AN.NA

5. *ku-nu-ku* 38 TÚG$^{\text{ḫi.a}}$

6. *Ú-ṣú-ur-ša-A-šùr ub-lá-ku-nu-tí*

7. *ig$^!$-ri sà-ri-dim ša-bu*

8. *mì-ma lá ta-da-na-šu-um*

9. *i-na pá-ni-im ṭup-pì-a áš-pu-ra-ku-nu-tí*

10. *um-ma a-na-ku-ma* AN.NA

11. *ù* TÚG$^{\text{ḫi.a}}$ / *a-na Ì-lí-a-lim*

12. *dí-na mì-ma la ta-da-na-šu-um*

13. *i-na ša šé-pì-šu* AN.NA

14. *ma-dam / il$_5$-ti-qí / i-na*

15. TÚG^{ḫi}*-tí-a / ma-aṭ-ú-tim*

Edge 16. *li-iq-a-ma / a-na ni-kà-sí-a*

Rev. 17. *qá-tí / i-ta-dí-a / ší-tí* TÚG^{ḫi}*-tí-a*

18. *ù* 2 GÚ AN.NA *a-na*

19. *A-šùr-⌈ta-⌉ak-lá-ku dí-na-ma*

20. *a-šar* KÙ.BABBAR 1 GÍN *Ba-lá-ṭá-a*

21. *lu-bi$_4$-il$_5$ / šu-ma lá-šu a-šar*

22. *wa-áš-bu šé-bi$_4$-lá-šu-um šu-ma*

23. *ḫa-ra-šu / a-n*[*i* AN.]NA-*ki*

24. *ù* TÚG^{ḫi}*-tí-*[*a a-na*] *ṣé-er*

25. DAM$^!$.GÀR [*ke-ni*]*m / a-na u$_4$-me*

26. *id-a* ⌈DAM.⌉GÀR *lu-ki-in*

27. *u$_4$-me* 1 ITI KAM *ù* 2 ITI KAM

28. *lá ta-ni$^!$-e-lá a-na Ì-lí-a-lim*

29. *qí-bi$_4$-ma ší-tí* KÙ.BABBAR *pá-ni-im*

30. 2 MA.NA *i-na pá-ni-im$^!$-ma*

Edge 31. *šé-bi$_4$-lam lu-qú-tám*

32. *ša šé-pí-kà za-ki-a-ma*

Left Edge 33. *tí-ib-a-ma a-<ta->al-kam ṭup-pu-um*

34. *a-ni-um wa-ar-ki*

Translation of Pa. 5 = L 29–558

(1) Thus (says) Asshur-īdī: (4) Speak to (2) Aḫ-Ishtar, Āl(i)-aḫum, Ilī-ālum (3) and Asshur-taklāku: (6) Uṣur-sha-Asshur carried (4) 2 talents (and) 1 mana of tin (5) (bearing) seals (and) 38 textiles (6) to you. (7) The pack master's wages are paid; (8) you should not pay him anything.

(9) I sent word to you in my earlier tablet (10) saying: (12) Give (10) the tin (11) and the textiles to Ilī-ālum, (so) (12) you should not give him anything (now). (14) He took much (13) tin from his caravan. (16) Take (15) the inferior ones (14) of (15) my textiles (16) and (17) deposit my portion (16) to my account. (19) Give (17) the rest of my textiles (18) and the 2 talents of tin to (19) Asshur-taklāku and (20) wherever (there is to be acquired) even one shekel of silver (21) let (20) Balaṭā bring (it). (21) If there is none (available where you are), then (22) send (it) to him (21) wherever (22) he is staying. If (23) his caravan is now (under way), (26) deposit (23) my tin (24) and my textiles to the account of (25) (a trustworthy) merchant for a specified period of time. (26) Let the merchant be trustworthy! (28) Do not become inattentive to this matter (27) for one or two whole months!

(29) Speak (28) to Ilī-ālum: (31) Send me (30) at the earliest opportunity (29) the rest of the first silver—2 manas. (32) Clear for me (31) the merchandise (32) of your caravan and (33) arise and come! (34) This (33) tablet (34) (is) my last (word)!

Notes on Pa. 5 = L 29–558

Line 2— The PN at the beginning of the line is clearly *A-aḫ-Ištar* after collation.

Line 5— One would expect *ku-nu-ki* as the plural, oblique case since the sealed tin must be the object of the verb *ublakkunūti*. The sign is clearly *ku*, however.

Line 15— Our rendering of *ma*-AD-*ú-tim* follows Veenhof (AOATT 202) who translates *ma-aṭ-ú-tim* as "of less good quality," instead of *ma-ad-ú-tim*, "many" in the sense of "additional." Had the latter expression been the scribe's intention, he should have written *ma*-DU-*ú-tim*.

Line 20— The PN *Ba-lá-ṭá-a* is not known to me elsewhere in OA. The verb, *balāṭum*, in OA PNs appears only rarely as in the PN *Ba-al-ṭù-šar* (ICK 1, 161:5; ICK 2, 128:x + 69; EL 145:21 [= CCT 1,

18a]; 235:6 [= BIN 4, 173]; and BIN 4, 40:2). *Ba* is certain after collation.

Lines 23–28— These lines are rendered by Veenhof (AOATT 407): ". . . entrust my tin and textiles to a trustworthy merchant for a fixed term (of credit). The merchant should be trustworthy; don't attach too much value to one or two months (longer credit)." The difficulty lies in line 28, where Veenhof reads *lá ta-be-e-lá*, which is a possible reading of the traces,  . Veenhof (AOATT 407) takes the verb *be'ālum* to mean "to stick to, attach (too) much value to" and produces several parallel examples to illustrate this use of *be'ālum*. See the note on Pa. 8:37. The remains might be read *ni*!, however, which would make the crux a G present, second person plural of *ni'ālum*, "to lie down, sleep." This verb appears in KTH 6:28 as *lu-na-al* and BIN 6, 1:7, *ašar ta-tí-ni-li-ni* (see GKT Section 96b). The sense of the statement in this case would be a warning not to grow inattentive to the matter at hand during the coming month or two, which is the critical period in the "firm's" economic affairs. After collation, the questionable sign seems to be a poorly made *ni* in which the first vertical wedge slipped a little to the left.

Line 25— Collation clearly shows DAM with the final *Winkelhaken* in place.

Line 26— Most of the DAM appears on the text.

Pa. 6 = L 29–559

1. *um-ma A-šur-i-dí-ma a-na A-šùr-na-da*
2. *Ì-lí-a-lim ù A-šur-ta-ak-lá-ku*
3. *qí-bi-ma / ma-áš-qal-tí a-na um-mì-a-ni-a*
4. *i-na Na-ar-ma-ak A-šur a-ša-qal*
5. 20 MA.NA KÙ.BABBAR *Ì-lí-a-lúm*
6. *li-ik-nu-kam ú* 8 MA.NA KÙ.BABBAR
7. *ša a-na ma-na-aḫ-tim a-na Ku-lí-li*
8. *ḫa-bu-lu šu-ut-ma li-ik-nu-kam*
9. *a-pu-tum A-šùr-ta-ak-lá-ku*
10. *lá i-ba-ri ṭur*$_4$*-da-ni-šu Ì-lí-a-lam*$_5$
11. *i-na da-áš-e ṭur*$_4$*-dam*
12. *a-na A-šùr-na-da qí-bi-ma*
13. KÙ.BABBAR 20 MA.NA *ú ma-lá* <*ša*> *ta-kà-šu-du*
14. *iš-tí A-šur-*⌜*ta-*⌝*ak-lá-ku*

15. *šé-bi-lam a-na-kam lu a-na* AN.NA
Edge 16. *lu a-na* URUDU *a-dí ta-lá-kà-ni*
17. *lá-dí a-pu-tum A-šur-ta-ak-lá-ku*
Rev. 18. *lá i-ba-ri a-šu-mì* AN.NA
19. *ša ta-áš-pu-ra-ni* 30 MA.NA AN.NA
20. *a-na qá-tí-kà a-dí-na-kum ša* 10 MA.NA
21. AN.NA KÙ.BABBAR *a-dí-na-kum* ŠU.NIGÍN 40 MA.NA
22. *a-šu-mì ša* É *Nu-ur*-ZU *ša ta-áš-pu-ra-ni*
23. *ú-za-kà-ma a-ša-pá-ra-kum*
24. *a-pu-tum* / *a-wa-at* / DINGIR$^{ḫi.a}$
25. *ú-ṣur* / *a-dí* 5 *ḫa-am-ší-šu ù* 6 *ší-ší-šu*
26. *pá-kà a-na* DINGIR / *ta-dí-in*
27. *lá tù-pá-šé-er* / *a-pu-tum*
28. *a-na ni-ki-iš-tim ša* DINGIR *i-ki-šu-kà*
29. *lá ta-tù-ar* / *ta-tù-ar-ma*
30. *ta-ḫa-liq a-ma-kam e ú-ša-tù-kà-ma*
31. *e ta-*⌜*tur*$_4$!⌝ *da-na-at*
32. DINGIR$^{ḫi.a}$ *lá ta-ma-ší a-na Ì-lí-a-lim*
33. *qí-bi-ma a-na*! *ša qí-ip-tám*
34. *ta-aq-tí-pu i-a-tí a-na ma-ga-ri-im*
Edge 35. *ta-ta-na-aḫ-ma ta-aq-tí-iš*
36. *i-a-am* / AN.NA-*ki ù* TÚG^{ḫi}-*tí-a*
Left Edge 37. *ša-ni-ú-tim ša-aq-tí-ni-pá a-ta*
38. *a-šar ša-nim tal-té-qé i-na kà-ri-im*
39. *tù-uk-ta-bi-id-ni*

Translation of Pa. 6 = L 29–559

(1) Thus (says) Asshur-īdī: to Asshur-nādā, (2) Ilī-ālum and Asshur-taklāku (3) speak. (4) I will weigh out (3) my payment (due) to my investor (4) in the month of Narmak Asshur. (5) Let Ilī-ālum (6) seal for me (5) 20 manas of silver. (6) Further (8) let him, himself, seal for me (6) the 8 manas of silver (7) which (8) he owes (7) to Kulili for expenses. (9) Pay attention! Shall Asshur-taklāku (10) not look (into the situation)? Send him! (11) Send (10) Ilī-ālum (11) in the springtime.

(12) Speak to Asshur-nādā (saying): (15) Send (14) with Asshur-taklāku (13) the silver—20 manas or as much as you have. (15) Here (17) let me deposit (it) (15) either for tin (16) or copper until you come.

(17) Pay attention! Shall Asshur-taklāku (18) not look (into the situation)?

(18) In regard to the tin (19) about which you wrote me, (20) I have given for you (19) 30 manas of tin (20) into your account (lit., hand). Concerning the 10 manas of (21) tin, I have given silver for you. Altogether 40 manas.

(22) Regarding the house of Nūr-Su'en about which you wrote me, (23) I will settle the matter and send word to you. (24) Pay attention! (25) Be vigilant about (24) the word of the gods! (25) Five and six times (26) you have pledged (given) your word to the gods! (27) May you not break (your word)! Pay attention! (29) You must not oppose (i.e., turn back against) (28) the fate which the gods have determined (for) you. (29) (If) you do oppose (it), (30) you are lost! Don't let me find you there and (31) don't you turn back! (32) You must not forget (31) the power of (32) the gods!

(33) Speak (32) to Ilī-ālum: (33) In regard to (34) your having entrusted (me) (33) (with) investment capital, (35) you have become tired of (34) managing (it) (35) and (so) you gave (it to me to manage). (37) Cause (someone) to invest (36) mine—my (37) other (36) tin and my (37) other (36) textiles. (39) You (37) yourself (39) have honored me (38) in the Mercantile Center (*kārum*) where you had taken (them) a second time.

Notes on Pa. 6 = L 29–559

Line 4— See Hirsch UAR 54 and J. Lewy ArOr 11 (1939) 38 for this MN.

Line 7— The name *Ku*-NI-*li* may be read *Ku-zal-li* as a MN or *Ku-lí-li*, a PN known from ICK 1, 130:10 (*Ku-li-li*) and numerous places in the form *Ku-li-lim*. The lack of ITI KAM before the name favors *Ku-lí-li* as a PN. The MN Kuzalli usually appears with either ITI KAM or ITI 1 KAM preceding it, but in three occurrences we discover the word *ku*-NI-*li* in circumstances which lead to ambiguity. The first of these three cases is VAT 9225:8–11 (see EL I, p. 222, n. a) which reads (8) 3 MA.NA KÙ.BABBAR (9) *i-na ku*-NI-*li a-ni-ú-tim* (10) *ša li-mì-im Aḫ-mar-ší* (11) *i-ša-qá-lá-am*. The CAD (K 613b), as well as von Soden (AHw 519a), takes the term to designate the MN even though it is modified by the plural demonstrative pronoun "these." The plural demonstrative pronoun suggests a plural, masculine, oblique reading for *ku*-NI-*li*. Three possibilities present themselves: *kuzallum*, "shepherd"; *guzallum*, "rogue, rascal"; and *guzalūm*, "chair-bearer," an official of some sort. None of these terms is attested in OA or makes much sense in VAT 9225, however. At any rate, the interpretation of *ku*-NI-*li* as a MN is highly questionable. In the second case, CCT 4, 32b:20–23, we find (20) 1 1/3 MA.NA 2 1/3 GÍN (21) KÙ.BABBAR *ù ṣí-ba-sú* (22) *ša iš-tù-ku*-NI-*li* (23) *šé-bi-lá-am*. *Ku*-NI-*li* in this context may be considered as the PN *Ku-lí-li*: (23) Bring me (20) the 1 1/3 manas (and) 2 1/3 shekels of (21) silver and its interest (22) which (comes) from Kulili. *Ku*-NI-*li* in ICK 2, 104:A 12 and B 12 likewise should be understood as a PN, *Ku-lí-li*. Since in every case but one (VAT 9225) *ku*-NI-*li*, when designating a MN, is preceded by ITI KAM or ITI 1 KAM, we favor *ku*-NI-*li* in the sense of a PN in Pa. 6:7.

Line 28— AHw 788b cites CCT 4, 1a:7 (*ana ni-ki-iš-tim ša ilim īṣirakkunni*) and suggests the root as *nakāsum*, "to cut off, fell" (AHw 720f.). Hirsch (UAR 4b) also treats this line in a similar way (*ana ni-ki-ís-tim ša ilū i-ṣí-ra-ku-ni*, "Auf die ≪Abschneidung≫, die der Gott dir einritzte, kehre nicht zurück!").

Line 30— *e ú-ša-tù-kà-ma* is probably to be taken as an Š of *atūm* (WTU), "to find," even though one would expect *ú-šé-tù-kà-ma*. Although there is no known example of the Š stem of this verb, CAD A_2 520 shows an Št stem.

Line 31— The *tur*$_4$ is too badly preserved to be completely secure.

Line 33— See Larsen OACP 73f. for *qīptum* as "the amount of money entrusted to a business partner for buying commodities for resale."

Line 35— *Ta-ta-na-aḫ-ma* comes from *anāḫum* in the sense of "to exert oneself, to have had enough of, be tired of"; CAD A_2 103a. In our context, however, the verb might make better sense as "to trouble." The troublesome lines would then run: (35) You have put the burden (34) on me to manage (it) (35) (by) giving (it to me) (literally, "and you gave [it to me]").

Line 38— Note *talteqe* for *talteqū* following *ašar*.

Pa. 7 = L 29–560

1. *um-ma Ša-lim-a-ḫu-um-ma a-na*
2. *Pu-šu-ki-in ù* ᵈNIN.ŠUBUR-*ba-ni*
3. *a-na* ᵈNIN.ŠUBUR-*ba-ni qí-bi*$_4$-*ma*

4. *i-na ṭup-pì-im ša Lá-qí-ip*
5. 6 1/3 MA.NA AN.NA *i-na*
6. *šu-uq-li-kà* ^{d}NIN.ŠUBUR-*ba-ni*
7. *il*$_{5}$-*qí-ma i-nu-mì-šu-ma a-na*
8. *Ḫa-tim i-ta-lá-ak ku-sí-tám*
9. *pá-ṣí-tám ša ik-ri-bi*$_{4}$-*a*
10. *Ì-lí-áš-ra-ni a-na A-šùr-ma-lik*
11. *ú-bi*$_{4}$-*il*$_{5}$ *A-šur-ma-lik ù-lá*
12. *ik-šu-ud i-ta-ṣa-am ku-sí-tám*
13. *a-ta tal-qí um-ma a-ta-ma*
14. *a-na a-bi*$_{4}$-*a šé-bu-lá-at*
15. 1/2 *ku-ta-nim ša šé-ep*
16. *Nu-ur-Ištar* 15 GÍN KÙ.BABBAR
17. *a-na Dan-A-šur ta-aq-bi*$_{4}$
18. *um-ma a-ta-ma wa-ar-kà-at-kà*

Edge 19. *ú-šé-ba-lam mì-ma a-nim*
20. *iš-tù li-mì-im Aḫ-mar-ší*

Rev. 21. *tù-kà-a-al tí-ir-tí*
22. *a-dí ḫa-am-ší-šu i-li-kà-*⸢*kum*⸣
23. *lu ša* AN.NA *ku-sí-tim*
24. *ù* 1/2 *ku-ta-nim* KÙ.BABBAR *a-na*
25. *Pu-šu-ki-in dí-in ù-lá*
26. *šu-up-ra-am-ma a-na-kam i-na*
27. KÙ.BABBAR-*pì-kà lá-al-qí*
28. 3 TÚG$^{ḫi.a}$ *ša ik-ri-*<*bi-*>*a*
29. 1 TÚG *ša ṣú-ḫa-ar-tim iš-tí*
30. *ṣú-ba-tí-kà A-šùr-ma-lik* DUMU *A-sú-a*
31. *ub-lá-kum* 1 MA.NA KÙ.BABBAR *a-na*
32. *Pu-šu-ki-in dí-in-ma a-li-bi*$_{4}$
33. KÙ.BABBAR-*pì-a li-dí ú-lá ta-áš-ta-na-me*
34. *ki-ma a-dí* KÙ.BABBAR-*pì-kà* 1 GÍN
35. *a-šar ni-du-nu ša-tí-ša-ma*
36. *iš-tí ṣa-bi*$_{4}$-*im* 5 *ù iš-ra-at*
37. *šu-t*[*a-a*]*l-mu-na-ku A-šùr*
38. [*u* ^{d}]NIN.ŠUBUR ⸢*li-*⸣*ṭù-lá*

Edge 39. *a-šar* [KÙ.BABBA]R 1 GÍN *a-dí-nu* KÙ.BABBAR-*pì*
40. 10 MA.NA *ù* 20 MA.NA
41. *lu i-ru-qá-ni*

Left Edge 42. *a-ḫi a-ta li-bi*$_{4}$ *lá tù-lá-ma-an* KÙ.BABBAR-*pì a-*⸢*na*⸣
43. *Pu-šu-ki-in dí-in ú-lá šu-up-ra-ma a-na-kam*
44. *i-na* KÙ.BABBAR-*pì-kà lá-al-qí li-bi*$_{4}$ *lá tù-lá-ma-an*

Translation of Pa. 7 = L 29–560

(1) Thus (says) Shalim-aḫum: (3) (Speak) to (2) Pūshu-kēn and Ilaprat-bāni. (3) To Ilaprat-bāni speak: (4) In (accordance with) Lā-qēp's tablet (6) Ilaprat-bāni (7) took (5) 6 1/3 manas of tin from (6) your package (7) and on the same day (8) went (7) to (8) Ḫattum. (10) Ilī-ashranni (11) brought (9) a white (8) mantle (10) to Asshur-malik (9) (as a part) of my *ikribū*-funds. (11) He did not (12) reach (11) Asshur-malik, (12) (for) he had left. (13) You took (12) the mantle. Thus you said, (14) (It is) for my father.

(14) (In regard to) the shipment of (15) one half (piece of) cloth of (16) Nūr-Ishtar's (15) caravan, (17) you promised (16) 15 shekels of silver (17) to Dan-Asshur. (18) Thus you said, After your departure (19) I will send (the silver).

(21) You have been holding (19) all this (20) since the eponymy of Aḫ(a)m-arshi. (22) As many as five times (21) my instructions (22) came to you! (23) Either (25) give (24) the silver (23) for the tin, the mantle, (24) and the half (piece of) cloth to (25) Pūshu-kēn or (26) write to me and (27) let me take (it) (26) from (27) your silver (26) here.

(30) Asshur-malik son of Asu'a (31) brought to you (28) 3 textiles of my *ikribū*-funds (and) (29) one young girl's textile along with (30) your textiles. (32) Give (31) one mana of silver to (32) Pūshu-kēn and (33) let him deposit (it) (32) into (33) my silver account.

(33) Don't you continually hear (34) that each year (37) I have trouble with (36) 5 or 10 persons (34) in regard to your silver (even as little as) one shekel (35) wherever we put (it)? (38) May (37) Asshur, [(38) and] Ilaprat behold! (39) Wherever I invest (give) silver (even as much as) one shekel, my silver (as much as) (40) 10 or 20 manas (41) flies from me! (42) You (are) my brother! Don't make my heart sick! (43) Give (42) my silver to (43) Pūshu-kēn! Do not send me a letter! Here (44) let me take some of your silver. Do not make my heart sick!

Notes on Pa. 7 = L 29–560

Lines 4–27 are treated by J. Lewy in OrNS 26 (1957) 19.

Line 6— On the weight of the *šuqlum* as approximately one talent, see H. Lewy RSO 39 (1964) 188, n. 2; J. Lewy HUCA 27 (1956) 32, n. 112; M. T. Larsen OACP 87f., 149, and 157, n. 75; and K. R. Veenhof AOATT 32, n. 66.

Lines 8f.— See Veenhof AOATT 160–162 for *kusītum paṣītum*, "a white *kusītum*-garment."

On Ḫattum as GN, see J. Lewy ArOr 18/3, part 4 (1950) 366–441; OrNS 26 (1957) 18–20; HUCA 32 (1961) 71 and B. Landsberger ArOr 18/3 (1950) 321–329.

Lines 9 and 28— *Ikribum*, usually appearing in the plural, represented precious metals and/or goods dedicated to a deity to be used as investment capital by business firms. *Ikribū*-funds were not subject to the *šaddu'ātum*-toll according to KTS 27b:13. BIN 6, 30:20 and CCT 4, 2a:3 show that *ikribū* of precious metal (silver in the latter text) were used to make a "sun(-disk)" for Asshur of one mana's weight. The comments in CAD I/J 66 suggest that the purpose of the *ikribū*-funds was to include the deity in their commercial enterprises in order to prosper from the deity's backing. J. Lewy felt that the *ikribū*-funds originated with the temple administration as loans to business firms (OrNS 26 [1957] 19, n. 2).

ICK 1, 12:B37–41 possibly suggests that the proceeds derived from investment of the *ikribū* went to underwrite a person among the cult personnel. "(37) 1 MA.NA (38) KÙ.BABBAR *ša ik-ri-bi*$_4$*-a ša I-ku-pí-a* (39) *ù-kà-lu* / *I-a-a* / *ú I-ku-pí-a* (40) *i-ma-ku-ru-ma* / *ik-ri-bi*$_4$*-a* / [*a-na*] (41) *me-er-i-tí* / *šu-nu-ma* / *e-ki-mu*[ ]: (39) Yaya and Ikū(n)-pīa (40) will manage (37) the one mana of (38) silver of my *ikribū*-funds which Ikū(n)-pīa (39) holds, (40) and (41) they will hold back (40) my *ikribū*-funds [for] (41) my daughter."

The daughter, Aḫatum, was a *gubabtum*-priestess, as seen in lines 9f. and 13, whose future was carefully provided for by her father, Ilībāni, in this, his will. Unfortunately, ICK 1, 12 does not indicate with which cult Aḫatum was associated. An Aḫatum is known from EL 58 (= KTS 45b) where she loaned 2/3 of a mana of silver at interest for 3 months, as well as EL 75 (= BIN 4, 153) where she loaned 1/3 of a mana also for 3 months. In EL 205 (= TC 2, 67), an Aḫatum and her husband Aḫuni son of Shu-Ishtar owe a debt-tablet to the DAM.GÀR. EL 214 (= BIN 4, 183) records the purchase of a slave by an Aḫatum. ICK 1, 27 A and B records the purchase of a girl from her parent by an Aḫatitum, perhaps the same name as Aḫatum. CCT 4, 15a shows an Aḫatum, together with a certain Mannu-kī-ēnī, addressed in a letter as *ummī* and *beltī*. MAH 16312 (published by Garelli in RA 59 [1965] 34f.) may be of significance in attempting to determine Aḫatum's religious connections. This text records the loan of a half mana of refined silver to a certain Lalum owing to Aḫatum following the standardized form. Added to the end, however, is the statement: "(18) I have given (15) all (16) this to (17) Lalum (in addition to the half mana)— (11) 6 shekels of silver for a *tadmiqtum* ("interest-free loan," according to Garelli) (13) additionally 1 1/2 shekels of (14) silver (as) the *ikribū* (15) of Asshur." If the Aḫatum of this text is the same Aḫatum of ICK 1, 12, we may conclude that Aḫatum was a *gubabtum*-priestess in the Asshur temple and that the *ikribū* arrangement was likewise a part of the investment procedures of the Asshur cult.

Other occurrences of *ikribū* in the Pennsylvania texts are 10:16, 19, and 13:22.

Line 18— For *wa-ar-kà-at-kà*, see GKT Section 102h. This example of suffixing an object to *warkatum* is the only one known to me.

Line 20— The *līmum* of *Aḫ-mar-ší* is previously known from VAT 9225: 10, published by J. Lewy in EL I 219, n. a on p. 222. A similar PN, *A-ḫa-na-ar-ší*, appears as the debtor in Chantre 16:3 (= EL 17) and its duplicate MAH 10825:3 (Garelli text no. 1, RA 59 [1965] 20).

Line 30— The PN *A-sú-a* father of Asshur-malik may be the same as *A-sí-a* in CCT 2, 2:29, 44; *A-sú* in EL 72:4 (= KTP 22) and 287:1, 8, 17, 27 (= Jena 369) and *A-sú-ú* in EL 152:4 (= Jena 387); and *A-sú* DUMU *Ma-n[a-na]* in CCT 6, 18b: 6.

Lines 36f.— These lines are understood this way in CAD L 118b.

Line 37— The *šu* at the beginning is clear on the tablet as shown by collation.

Line 38— The *li* of *li-ṭù-lá* is clear from collation. Nothing is missing at the beginning of the line but *u*.

Pa. 8 = L 29–561

1. *a-na A-šùr-na-da Ú-ṣú-ur-ša-A-šùr*
2. *ù I-dí-*ZU.IN *qí-bi*$_4$*-ma*
3. *um-ma Ì-lí-a-lúm-ma* 2 1/2 MA.NA
4. KÙ.BABBAR *ṣa-ru-pu-um* 10 1/6 GÍN KÙ.GI
5. *ba-ša-lúm ša áb-ni-šu ku-nu-ki-a*
6. *I-dí-A-šùr kà-ṣa-ar A-al-*DU$_{10}$ *ub-lá-ku-nu-tí*
7. 12 5/6 MA.NA 7 GÍN KÙ.BABBAR *ṣa-ru-pá-am*
8. 1/3 MA.NA 7 GÍN KÙ.GI *ku-nu-ki*
9. *ša Kur-ub-Ištar ù A-mur-Ištar Be-lúm-ba-ni*

10. *ub-lá-ku-nu-tí* 5 MA.NA KÙ.BABBAR *ṣa-ru-pá-am*
11. *ku-nu-ki-a* / *A-šùr-ta-ak-lá-ku*
12. DUMU *A-bu-Ša-lim* / *na-áš-a-ku-nu-tí*
13. ŠU.NIGÍN 20 1/3 MA.NA 7 GÍN KÙ.BABBAR
14. *ù* 1/2 MA.NA 7 1/6 GÍN KÙ.GI *i-li-kà-ku-nu-tí*
15. [ŠÀ.]BA 15 1/2 MA.NA KÙ.BABBAR *a-na*
16. *Pu-šu-ki-in šu-uq-lá-ma ṭup-pì*
17. *li-dí-na-ku-nu-tí ší-tí* KÙ.BABBAR *ù* KÙ.GI
18. *a-na A-šùr-na-da dí-na-ma a-na*
19. *lu-qú-tí-šu li-ku-ul a-na ṣé-er*
20. KÙ.BABBAR *pá-ni-im ù tí-ir-ta-ku-nu*
Edge 21. *li-li-kam* 9 GÚ URUDU SIG$_5$
22. 5$^?$ MA.NA 6 GÍN KÙ.BABBAR *ṣa-ru-pu-*⌜*um*⌝
Rev. 23. *a-na Ú-ṣú-ur-ša-A-šùr ù*
24. *I-dí-*ZU.IN *I-dí-A-šùr En-nam-Be-lúm*
25. *ù I-šar-Be-lúm iš-tù*
26. *da-áš-e ú-šé-bi$_4$-lá-ku-nu-tí*
27. ŠÀ.BA 10 MA.NA KÙ.BABBAR *a-na Šu-Be-lim i-ší-qí-il$_5$*
28. 35 *maš-ki* 18 ^{túg}*pì-ri-kà-ni*
29. *I-dí-A-šùr ù En-nam-Be-lúm a-na*
30. *ša ki-ma i-a-tí i-dí-nu ṭup-pá-am*
31. *na-áš-pá-ar-tám ú-lá ub-lu-nim um-ma*
32. *I-dí-A-šùr-ma lá-pá-tám lá i-mu-ú*
33. *a-ba-ú-a* / *a-tù-nu* URUDU-*i ma-lá ta-*⌜*ad-*⌝*nu*
34. *ší-im maš-ki ù pì-ri-kà-ni* / *ma-lá it-bu-lu-*[*ni*]
35. *ší-tí* KÙ.BABBAR / *ma-lá i-ší-ta-ni tí-ir-ta-ku-nu*
36. *a-na Du-ur-ḫu-mì-id li-li-kam*
37. 20 MA.NA <URUDU> SIG$_5$ *a-na I-dí-A-šùr a-na be-a-lim*
38. *a-dí* / *ú ma-lá* URUDU *ba-lúm tí-ir-tí-a I-dí-*ZU.IN
39. *a-na I-dí-A-šùr a-na ší-a-ma-tim*
40. *a-na Ḫu-ra-ma iš-pu-ru i-ma-lá i-dí-nu-šu-ni*
41. *ù be-ú-lá-tí-šu e-lá* 1 GÚ 1 MA.NA
42. URUDU *ṣa-ḫi-ri-im ù* 1 ^{túg}*pì-ri-kà-nim*
43. *mì-ma a-na ša ki-ma i-a-tí ú-lá i-dí-in*
44. *I-dí-A-šùr iš-tí-a ú-lá i-na-me-er*
45. *a-ma-kam lu-ba-li-ṭá-ku-nu-tí*
Edge 46. *a-na I-dí-*ZU.IN *qí-bi$_4$-ma A-šùr lu i-dí*
47. *i-na ṣé-er ša pá-ni-tim tù-uš-ta-áb-ri-am*
48. *mì-šu-um* URUDU *a-na I-dí-A-*<*šur*>
49. *tù-šé-er ù* URUDU *tù-ma-li Ḫa-šu-dar i-na* [*Kà-*]*ni-*⌜*iš*⌝
wa-ša-⌜*áb*⌝

50. *a-ta a-na Tí-mì-il$_5$-ki-a té-tí-iq-ma* x *tap-pá-*[*ú-*]*šu i-dí-nu-ni-ku-ma*
51. *a-wi-lam tù-ta-ší-ir-ma* KÙ.BABBAR *ṭù-ur-dí eq-lam* ⌜*im-*⌝[ ]*-ma*
52. *a me*! x *ta-áš-ku-na-ni*

Translation of Pa. 8 = L 29–561

(2) Speak (1) to Asshur-nādā, Uṣur-sha-Asshur, (2) and Īdī-Su'en. (3) Thus (says) Ilī-ālum: (6) Īdī-Asshur, the caravan leader of Āl-ṭāb, brought to you (3) 2 1/2 manas of (4) refined silver (and) 10 1/6 shekels of (5) smelted (4) gold (5) ore (bearing) my seals. (9) Bēlum-bāni (10) brought to you (7) 12 5/6 manas (and) 7 shekels of refined silver (and) (8) 1/3 of a mana (and) 7 shekels of gold (bearing) the seals (9) of Kurub-Ishtar and Amur-Ishtar. (11) Asshur-taklāku (12) son of Abu-Shalim is carrying to you (10) 5 manas of refined silver (11) (bearing) my seals. (13) Altogether 20 1/3 manas (and) 7 shekels of silver (14) and 1/2 of a mana (and) 7 1/6 shekels of gold have gone to you. (15) From this amount (16) weigh out (15) 15 1/2 manas of silver to (16) Pūshu-kēn and (17) let him give (16) tablets (17) to you. (18) Give (17) the rest of the silver and gold (18) to Asshur-nādā and (19) let him hold (it) (18) for (19) his goods. (It is to be added) onto (20) the earlier silver. Then (21) let (20) your instructions (21) come to me.

(24) Īdī-Asshur, Ennam-Bēlum (25) and Ishtar-Bēlum (26) sent for you (21) 9 talents of good-quality copper (and) (22) 5 manas (and) 6 shekels of refined silver (23) to Uṣur-sha-Asshur and (24) Īdī-Su'en (25) after (26) spring. (27) From this amount 10 manas of silver have been weighed out to Shū-Bēlum. (29) Īdī-Asshur and Ennam-Bēlum (30) gave (28) 35 hides and 18 *pirikannū*-textiles (29) to (30) my representative.

(31) Did they not bring to me a message (30) tablet (with the following message)? (32) Thus Īdī-Asshur (said), They do not want to write! (33) You (are) my "fathers." (36) Let (35) your instructions (36) come to me at Durḫumid (regarding) (33) whatever you have sold (of) my copper, (34) the price of the hides and the *pirikannū*-textiles whatever they "brought" (that is, cost), (and) (35) whatever is left over of the rest of the silver.

(38) I have deposited (37) 20 manas of good(-quality) copper for Īdī-Asshur to invest. (43) He has not given anything whatever to my representative, (38) either any copper (which) Īdī-Su'en without my

instructions [40] wrote [39] to Īdī-Asshur [40] at Ḫurrama [39] for (making) purchases—[40] from whatever he gave him—[41] nor (did he give) his interest-free investment capital except one talent (and) one mana of [42] copper in small pieces, nor (did he give) one piece of *pirikannum*-textile. [44] Īdī-Asshur has not met me. [45] Let him credit (the proper amount) to you there.

[46] Speak to Īdī-Su'en: Asshur surely knows (that) [47] on the earlier (load) you have caused an inspection to be made. [48] Why [49] did you release [48] the copper to Īdī-Asshur(!) [49] and (why) did you load up the copper? Ḫashudar is residing in Kanish(!). [50] You went over to Timilkia and [51] you freed the gentleman [50] of that which his partner had given to you. [51] Therefore send me the silver! (The rest is too fragmentary to attempt a translation.)

Notes on Pa. 8 = L 29–561

Lines 4f.— KÙ.GI BA-*ša-lum ša abnišu.* This expression is treated by Veenhof (AOATT 57, n. 103) and taken to mean "electrum 'from ore.'"

Von Soden (AHw 841) understands the adjective BA-*ša-lum* as *pašallum* even though the verb "to cook, ripen" begins with "b." CAD B 135ff. includes among additional meanings for *bašālum*, "to melt, boil"; the CAD apparently intends to include BA-*šallum* in the P volume, however, since it does not appear in the B volume. AHw finds no etymology with which to associate its *pašallum*. The initial "p" seems to be preferred because the later spellings where "b" and "p" are distinguished use *pa*, not *ba*. Hecker (GKT Section 54e) questions whether *pašallum* is a Semitic word. Garelli (AC 268, n. 3) associates *pašallum* and *pašlum* (sic!).

Line 6— *Kaṣṣārum* is translated "freighter" by Veenhof (AOATT 86f.) rather than "harnessor" since the *kaṣṣārum* accompanied the caravan en route and might receive *be'ulātum*-funds as working capital. We will translate it "caravan leader" throughout.

Lines 13f.— The scribe's arithmetic is correct.

Lines 28 and 34— *Pirikannū*-textiles (also in line 42) are judged to be native products in OACP 44, n. 1 and AOATT 124–128, which could be made into cloths. Veenhof's results show that *pirikannū* were made of wool and were probably coarse in texture since they were less expensive than Mesopotamian textiles. They were not imported into

Assyria and were an intra-Anatolian trade commodity of significance. *Pirikannum* appears also in Pa. 21:20, 22; 26:12; and 29:18.

Lines 34f.— rendered by Veenhof (AOATT 440). *Tabālum* here means "to bring" in the sense of "to cost." See OACP 31.

I-ší-ta-ni is to be derived from *ši'ātum*, "to have or keep a remainder" (GKT Sections 78f and 94), and is to be seen as a feminine, plural subjunctive of the G stem. In our context the verb must have the intransitive meaning of "to be left over."

Line 36— Durḫumid is to be located somewhere north of Kanish (i.e., Kültepe). See Garelli AC 110 and 121f.; Goetze *Kleinasien*, Second Edition, 72; J. Lewy HUCA 27 (1956) 64–66; and H. Lewy JCS 17 (1963) 103.

Line 37— For the meaning of URUDU SIG_5, see AOATT 194f.

For the OA use of the verb *be'ālum*, "to have power over money or property," see CAD B 201 and AHw 121a. Veenhof (AOATT 407–412) has further defined the verb in several idiomatic uses. The associated noun, *be'ulātum* in line 41, is now understood as "an interest-free loan . . . to be used for private business, in order to earn . . . wages" (AOATT 407). See also J. Lewy OrNS 29 (1960) 23, n. 3 and OACP 41, 149f.

Line 39— For *ši'amātum*, "purchases," see OACP 44, 153 and GKT Sections 59g and 64g.

Line 40— Veenhof locates Ḫurrama as the "only town between Timilkia and Shalatuwar" (AOATT 313). J. Lewy (HUCA 32 [1961] 68, n. 210 and HUCA 33 [1962] 45–57) located Ḫurrama "in the vicinity of Elbistan, about 150 kilometers southeast of Kültepe." See Goetze's map in *Kleinasien*, Second Edition, 54f. This GN appears also in Pa. 19:29.

Line 41— *e lá* may be taken several ways: 1) *ela* = "over, above, more than" (GAG Section 114o); 2) *ela* = "besides, apart from" (CAD E 73f.); or 3) *ē lā* = the double negative in the possible meaning of "absolutely, no less than" (see GKT Section 105a and J. Lewy OrNS 29 [1960] 32, n. 4).

Line 42— Veenhof (AOATT 431, n. 547) reads: 1 GÚ URUDU *ṣa-ḫi-ri-im* omitting 1 MA.NA and comments that *ṣaḫḫirum* might be compared with *šabburum*, "broken," in describing copper.

Line 47— The reading is verified by CCT 3, 44a:16–18: *i-ṣé-er ša pá-ni-a-tí-im* URUDU-*a-ni tù-uš-ta-áb-ri-am*. Otherwise the usage is unknown to me. The verbal form appears to be an Št of *barā'um*, "to look upon, observe, inspect"; this is therefore the only attested Š form for the OA dialect. The last vertical wedge of *ta* is clearly preserved on the text.

Line 48— The end of the line may be read *I-dí-A-*<*šur*> or *i-a-tí* by metathesis. A scribal mistake is possible since the scribe was squeezing the writing to get everything on the tablet.

Line 49— The PN *Ḫa-šu-dar* is unknown to me elsewhere.

Line 50— The traces favor UB TAB BA [ ] ŠU, which makes no sense. The collation notes of H. and J. Lewy suggest the reading *ša tap-pá-*[*ú-*]*šu iddinūnikum*(*a*), "that which his partner(s) had given to you . . ." Collation shows the *ša* to be doubtful.

Line 51— If the reading *eq-lam* is correct, as it appears after collation, we should expect some form of the verbs *alākum* or *etāqum* to appear in the lacuna. Collation, however, has not resolved the question.

Line 52— The opening of this line on the basis of Mrs. Lewy's drawing may be read in several ways: 1) *a-lá-am*! *taškunanni*, "you have set down for me the City (of Assur)"; 2) *a lā* ÈR! *taškunanni* = *lā ana wardim taškunanni*, "you have not made me into a slave" or "have you not made me into a slave?"; or 3) *a lā* LÚ! *taškunanni* = *lā ana awilim taškunanni*, "you have not made me into a gentleman" or "have you not made me into a gentleman?" The poor state of preservation makes it impossible to determine what the writer's intention was.

Collation suggests that the sign Mrs. Lewy saw as *lá* should be taken as *me*, 𒈨 . There is room for the horizontal wedge to be written higher if the scribe intended to write *lá*. What follows the *me* is not clear. I suggest *tim* and read *a me-tim taškunanni*: "you have made me (as good as) a dead man."

Pa. 9 = L 29–562

1. *Da-na-a* / *wu-ba-ar-tám*
2. *im-ḫu-ur-ma* GÍR
3. *ú-šé-ṣí-ma um-ma Da-na-a-ma*
4. *a-na Ma-na-na-ma*
5. *a-na ší-bu-tim ú-lá áš-ku-kà*
6. *a-na a-i-tim ṭup-pá-am*
7. *ša ší-bu-tí-kà ta-dí-in*
8. *um-ma Ma-na-na-ma*
9. *ú-lá wa-dí-a-ma* / *ṭup-pá-am*

10. *a-dí-in / a-wi-lúm*
11. *kà-ra-am / Ta-wi-ni-a*
12. *im-ḫu-ur-ni-a-tí-ma*

Edge 13. *kà-ru-um i-dí-ni-a-tí-ma*

Rev. 14. *a-na-ku ù tap-pá-i*

15. *ṭup-pá-am ni-dí-in*
16. *um-ma Ma-na-na-ma i-nu-mì*
17. *ṭup-pá-am ba-áb /* DINGIR
18. *ni-dí-nu ⌜a-⌝wa-tim*
19. *ša a-na-ku / lá i-dí-ú*
20. *ší-ta ù ša-lá-áš*
21. *tap-pá-i / ú-ḫa-sí-sà-ni-ma*
22. *ù qá-sú ú-ša-ší-šu-ma*
23. *a-wa-tim ša ú-ḫa-sí-sá-ni-ni*
24. *nu-ra-dí / um-ma Da-na-a-ma*
25. *a-na ší-bu-tim*

Edge 26. *ú-lá áš-ku-kà um-ma*

27. *Ma-na-na-ma / ki-na*

Left Edge 28. *a-na ší-bu-tim / ú-lá ta-áš-ku-ni*

29. *ù i-nu-mì / ṭup-pá-am*
30. *ni-dí-nu ší-bu-*tam_4 */ mì-ma*
31. *ú-lá nu-dí ṭup-pu-um a-num*
32. *ša ba-áb /* DINGIR

Translation of Pa. 9 = L 29–562

(1) Danā (2) came before (1) the "Colony" (*wubartum*) (2) and (3) he caused (2) the dagger (3) to be brought out, and thus (said) Danā (4) to Manana: (5) I did not appoint you for (bearing) witness. (6) Why (then) did (7) you give (6) a tablet (7) recording (i.e., of) your testimony, (8) saying (lit., thus (said) Manana), (9) I was not informed and (so) (10) I gave (9) a tablet? (10) The gentleman (12) came before (11) the Mercantile Center (*kārum*) of Tawinia (12) for us and (13) the Mercantile Center (*kārum*) rendered (judgment) for us and (14) I and my partner (15) have given a tablet.

(16) Thus (says) Manana, When (18) we gave (17) the tablet at the gate of the god, (21) my partner informed me (20) two or three times (18) of a matter (19) (about) which I did not know (anything) (21) and (22) so I caused him to take an oath (i.e., to raise his hand) and (24) we added on (23) the matter of which he informed me.

(24) Thus (says) Danā, (26) I did not appoint you (25) for (bearing) witness.

(26) Thus (says) (27) Manana, (It is) true; (28) you did not appoint me for (giving) testimony. (29) Moreover when (30) we gave (29) the tablet, (31) we did not make known (30) any testimony.

(31) This tablet (is) (32) that of the gate of the god.

Notes on Pa. 9 = L 29–562

Line 1— For *wa/ubartum* = "colony," see J. Lewy HUCA 27 (1956) 59–64. The known *wubarātum* are listed in n. 251 on p. 59. J. Lewy saw the term as a collective from *ubārum*, "resident alien, emigrant" (n. 252 on p. 60) and, therefore, preferred the reading *wubartum* over *wabartum*.

Line 2— Collation shows the vertical wedge at the end of GÍR is on the text, though it has only a short tail.

Lines 4, 8, 16, and 27— The PN *Ma-na-na* (clearly beginning with *ma* and not *ku*) is also known from ICK 2, 45:A x + 19; KTH 19:2 as the father of Amurrum-bāni and Puzur-Sadū'e); TuM 1, 353:B 3 B 3 (father of Ennum-Asshur); and TC 1, 71:3 (father of Urā). Garelli's reading of *Ku-na-na* in MAH 19616:10 (RA 59 [1965] 47f.) should possibly be corrected to *Ma-na-na* in the light of the spellings in these other citations. We may possibly add CCT 6, 18b:6 where we find É *A-sú* DUMU *Ma-n[a-na]*.

Line 5— *Áš-ku-kà* = *aškunka*.

Line 6— *Ana a-i-tim*, "for what?" see CAD A_1 234ff. and GKT Section 51b.

Line 9— *Ula wa-dí-a-ma*. See GKT Section 97d.

Line 18— The *a* of *awātim* is preserved though damaged.

Lines 21 and 23— *Ú-ḫa-sí-sà-ni-ma* as a D stem of *ḫasāsum* must have the meaning of "to inform" in our text.

Line 22— *Ú-ša-ší-šu-ma* is an Š preterite of *našā'um*.

Line 24— *Nu-ra-dí* is a D form from *radā'um* which Hecker (GKT Sections 78a, d, and 95) understands to mean "to escort." AHw 967 takes the D stem of *radā'um* to mean "to add," which meaning makes better sense in our context.

Line 28— The end of the line is inscribed  .

Line 29— The first of the line is to be read *ù* 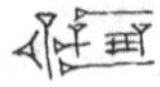 and not as Mrs. Lewy drew.

Lines 31f.— On the "tablet of the gate of the god," see Hirsch UAR 38f., n. 193.

Pa. 10 = L 29–563

	1.	*um-ma A-šùr-i-dí-ma*
	2.	*a-na A-šùr-na-da*
	3.	*qí-bi$_4$-ma / ra-ma-kà*
	4.	*za-ki-a-ma / tí-ib-a-ma*
	5.	*a-ta-al-kam*
	6.	*a-šu-mì ḫa-ra-ni-kà*
	7.	DINGIR / *li-ba-tí-kà*
	8.	*ma-li / ú šu-ma*
	9.	KÙ.BABBAR 1 GÍN *ma-ma-an*
	10.	*a-na na-ru-qí-im*
Edge	11.	*i-dá-na$^!$-ku-um*
Rev.	12.	*na-an-ší-am*
	13.	*ša-am-ša-am / ša*
	14.	1 MA.NA KÙ.GI
	15.	*a-na A-šùr ḫa-bu-lá-ku*
	16.	*i-na ik-ri-bi$_4$-a*
	17.	*ep-ša-am* 6 MA.NA
	18.	KÙ.BABBAR *a-na ^{d}Ištar*
	19.	*i-na li-bi$_4$ ik-ri-bi$_4$-a*
	20.	*be-lam šu-ma lá ma-ṣí*
	21.	*i-na ra-mi-ni-kà*
	22.	*i-dí / a-na šu-mì-kà*
	23.	*ak-ru-ub*
Edge	24.	*al-kam-ma*
Left Edge	25.	*a-ḫi-kà a-na wa-ar-du-≪du-≫tim*
	26.	*lá a-dí-na-ku-um*

Translation of Pa. 10 = L 29–563

(1) Thus (says) Asshur-īdī: (3) Speak (2) to Asshur-nādā, (saying), (4) Prepare (3) yourself (4) and arise and (5) come here! (6) Because of your caravan, (7) the god (8) is full of (7) anger against you. (8) So if (9) anyone (11) gives to you (9) silver (amounting even to) one shekel (10) for a *naruqqum*-sack, (12) take (it) for me. (15) I owe to Asshur

(13) a sun-disk of (14) one mana of gold. (17) Make (it) for me (16) from my *ikribū*-funds. (20) Bring (17) 6 manas of (18) silver to Ishtar (19) from my *ikribū*-funds. (20) If there is not a sufficient amount, (22) deposit (it) (21) from your own (funds). (23) I have offered prayers (22) for your sake (i.e., name). (24) Come here, for (26) I have not sold (25) your brother into slavery (26) on your account!

Notes on Pa. 10 = L 29–563

Line 4— See CAD Z 31 for the meaning "to make ready for departure."

Lines 6–8— See also CCT 4, 2a:26f. (another letter of Asshur-īdī to Asshur-nādā) for this same expression. The *ba* in *libbātum* is sure although carelessly written.

Line 11— The *na* is there; the horizontal wedges before the last vertical are faint but still visible.

Line 12— For *na-an-ší-am* as an N imperative with the meaning "to carry away, receive, transport personally," see GKT Sections 84c and 97c as well as AHw 765b.

Line 13— For *ša-am-ša-am* ("sun[disk], gold"), a divine emblem here made of one mana of gold and given to the national god, Asshur, see Hirsch UAR 66f.

Lines 16 and 19— For *ikribū*, see the notes on Pa. 7:9, 28.

Line 20— The *lam* is tilted upward and looks strange, but it is still *lam*.

Line 22— For *i-dí* as the imperative of *nadā'um*, see GKT Section 97c.

Line 23 has a long horizontal wedge at the end which appears to have no meaning.

Line 24— *Al-kam* = *alik* + *am* (imperative plus ventive). See MAH 16209:8 (RA 59 [1965] 156–160); KTK 20:18; KUG 38:22; ATHE 59:27; and EL 336:8, x + 1 (= KTH 33).

Line 25— The scribe started the *du* of *wardūtim* at the end of the line, then decided he did not have room to finish it, partially erased it, and wrote *du-tim* at the end of the next line.

Pa. 11 = L 29–564

1. *a-na E-dí-na-a ú A-šur-e-nam*
2. *qí-bi-ma um-ma En-nam-A-šur-ma*

3. *a-na A-šur-e-nam qí-bi-ma*
4. *ša-zu-úz-tum ša a-bi-a a-ta*!
5. 1/3 MA.NA 5 GÍN KÙ.BABBAR *iš-tí*
6. *Ili$_5$-ba-ni* DUMU *I-ku-nim*
7. *a-na ṣí-ib-tim ni-il$_5$-qí-ma*
8. *a-na Šu-Ištar a-na ḫu-bu-ul*
9. *a-bi-a ni-iš-qú-ul ṣí-ib-tám*
10. *ša* 2 *ša-na-at áš-qú-ul-ma*
11. *a-na* 1/3 MA.NA 5 GÍN KÙ.BABBAR

Edge 12. *ší-im-tim Ili$_5$-ba-ni / ta-pu-ul*
13. *ta-sí-ḫi-ir-ma*
14. *i-na ba-áb*

Rev. 15. *ḫa-ra-nim ṭup-pì*
16. *ša* 1/3 MA.NA 5 GÍN KÙ.BABBAR
17. *ta-al-pu-ut a-bi*
18. *i-li-kà-ma* KÙ.BABBAR
19. *Ili$_5$-ba-ni / uš-ta-bi-ma*
20. *a-ta ṭup-pá-am / ša ku-nu-ki-a*
21. *tù-kà-a-al / a-ma-kam*
22. *ṭup-pá-am / a-na a-bi-a*
23. *dí-in-ma / li-du-uk*
24. *a-bi a-ta / ṭup-pá-am*
25. *ša ku-nu-ki-a / a-na a-bi-a*

Edge 26. *dí-in-ma li-⌜du-⌝uk*

Translation of Pa. 11 = L 29–564

(2) Speak (1) to Edinā and Asshur-ennam. (2) Thus (says) Ennam-Asshur: (3) Speak to Asshur-ennam: (4) You (are) my father's representative. (7) We took (5) 1/3 of a mana (and) 5 shekels of silver from (6) Ilī-bāni son of Ikūnum (7) as interest and (9) we weighed (it) out (8) to Shū-Ishtar for the debt of (9) my father. (10) I have weighed out (9) the interest (10) accumulated over (i.e., of) 2 years and (12) you have paid off Ilī-bāni's contract (11) for 1/3 of a mana (and) 5 shekels of silver. (13) You came back and (17) wrote (15) tablets (16) for the 1/3 of a mana (and) 5 shekels of silver (14) on (your) departure with (15) the caravan. (17) My father (18) came and (19) Ilī-bāni has been completely paid (i.e., satisfied in regard to) (18) the silver, (19) and (20) you (21) hold (20) the tablet (bearing) my seals. (21) There (23) give (22) the tablet to my father (23) and let him destroy (it). (24) You (are) my "father."

(26) Give (24) the tablet (25) (bearing) my seals to my father (26) and let him destroy (it).

Notes on Pa. 11 = L29–564

Line 7— The *na* in *ana* is perfect on the tablet.

Line 13— *Ta-sí-ḫi-ir-ma* is the N stem of *saḫārum*, "to turn oneself around, come back." The *sí* is secure.

Line 19— Whether this D form of *šabā'um* with the infixed "t" is to be taken as a D perfect or as a D passive is debatable. If a D perfect, the clause would mean "he ("my father") has completely satisfied Ilī-bāni with silver"; if a D passive, "Ilī-bāni (the subject of the verb) has been completely satisfied with silver." In either case, the debt has obviously been paid and the matter settled.

Lines 23 and 26— The *uk* is squeezed at the end of line 23 but properly written at the end of line 26.

Lines 24–26— Note that the writer, Ennam-Asshur, thinks in terms of having two "fathers." This phraseology is ambiguous since *abum*, "father," has two distinct uses in these OA business documents, that is, progenitor and "boss." Our text might imply that Asshur-ennam, the addressee, is Ennam-Asshur's "boss," while the unnamed "father" in line 25 is his physical father. Also the possibility that Ennam-Asshur had two "bosses" cannot be completely ruled out.

Pa. 12 = L 29–566

1. *i-na* 14 1/2? MA.NA KÙ.BABBAR
2. *ša* 2 *ṭup-pè-e*
3. *ša E-dí-na-a ù*
4. *Ku-ra-ra a-na A-lá-ḫi-im*
5. *ù A-šùr-na-da ḫa-bu-lu-ni*
6. 3 MA.NA 15 GÍN KÙ.BABBAR
7. *ṣa-ru-pá-am E-dí-na-a-a*
8. *iš-tù ḫa-mu-uš-tim*
9. *ša Šu-Ku-bi*$_4$*-im ú Zu-pá*
10. *a-na* 7 *ḫa-am-ša-tim*
11. *i-ša-qal-ma ṭup-pá-am*
12. *ša ku-nu-ki-ni*

Edge 13. *ni-da-šu-um*
14. [KÙ.BABBAR?] *ša mì-iš-li-šu*
15. [*u-*]*ša-be-ú-ni-a-tí-ma*
Rev. 16. [ ]x *ša Ku-ra-ra*
17. [x *K*]*u-ra-ra ni-šé-e ú*
18. *šu-ma lá iš-qú-ul*
19. *ṭup-pu-um a-num*
20. *i-mu-at-ma*
21. 6 MA.NA 15 GÍN
22. *E-dí-na-a i-ša-qal*
23. *ù Ku-ra-ra a-qá-tí-šu*
24. *ni-šé-e* [*i-*]*na qá-*⌜*qá-*⌝*ad*
25. *šál-mì-šu-nu*
26. *ra-ak-sú ší-tí*
27. ⌜KÙ.BABBAR?-⌝*ma*? *ni-šé-e-šu-nu*

Translation of Pa. 12 = L 29–566

(7) Edinā (11) will weigh out (6) 3 manas (and) 15 shekels of (7) refined (6) silver (8) (counting) from the *ḫamushtum*-period (9) of Shū-Kubum and Zuppa (10) within 7 *ḫamushtum*-periods (1) from the 14 1/2(?) manas of silver (2) recorded on (lit., of) 2 tablets (3) which Edinā and (4) Kurara (5) owe (4) to Al(i)-aḫum (5) and Asshur-nādā, (11) and (13) we will give to him (11) a tablet (12) (bearing) our seals. (15) They will pay us (14) [the silver(?)] of his half (15) and (17) we will lay claim [x] Kurara (16) [. . .] of Kurara. (17) But (18) if he has not weighed (it) out, (19) this tablet (20) will be null (lit., die) and (22) Edinā will weigh out (21) 6 manas (and) 15 shekels. (23) But (as for) Kurara, (24) we will lay claim (23) to (or, for) his share. (26) They (the 6 manas and 15 shekels) are bound (24) on the head of (25) their guarantor. (27) We will lay claim against them (26) (for) the rest of (27) the silver(?).

Notes on Pa. 12 = L 29–566

Line 1— The 14 1/2 perhaps should be read 12 1/2.

Line 4— For the PN Al(i)-aḫum, see Pa. 5:2 above.

Line 7— J. Lewy traced the PN Edinā to the verbal form *iddina(m)*, "he has given me." See EL I 229, n. b.

Lines 8f.— The *ḫamuštum*-period of Šū-Kubum and Zuppa is not known to me elsewhere. Garelli (AC 148) takes Zuppa as Hittite.

Line 13— *Ni-da-šu-um* = *niddanšum*. The traces at the beginning of H. Lewy's line drawing are to be disregarded. Nothing is missing at the beginning of the line.

Lines 14–17— Line 16 is most uncertain. The traces at the beginning may be those of *na* which would suggest either of the prepositions *ina* or *ana*. We should, however, consider the possibility that the partial sign may be KI. Mrs. Lewy read *ana ša Kurara*: "as for that (half) of Kurara . . ."

There appears to be space for only one sign at the beginning of line 17. Mrs. Lewy, however, restored nothing in the lacuna.

Lines 17, 24, and 27— For the form *ni-šé-e*, see now AHw 1223a where it is taken as a G present of *še'ā'um* with the sense of "to demand, claim something from someone." See also GKT Section 98.

Line 21— Note that the amount due rises from 3 manas and 15 shekels to 6 manas and 15 shekels if the loan is not repaid on time.

Line 25— *Šalmišunu*, "their sound/well one," refers to someone who is economically solvent and able to act as guarantor of the money owed.

Line 26— The next-to-last sign which Mrs. Lewy drew as *ší* may be read as *ba*; the tail of the internal wedge is completely absent. BA.DI seems to make no sense in the context, however.

Line 27— The signs before *ni* are not clarified by collation; the one just ahead of the *ni* might be *ma* which was partially dulled before the tablet hardened. It is definitely not DIRIG = *watrum*. The tentative restoration of KÙ.BABBAR rests mainly on reading *ší-tí* at the end of line 26, which after collation is not completely certain. However, collation has not offered any preferable alternative.

Pa. 13 = L 29–567

1. *um-ma A-šur-i-dí-ma*
2. ⌜*a*-⌝*na A-šur-na-da*
3. *qí-bi$_4$-ma mì-šu*
4. *ša ta-áš-pu-ra-ni*
5. *um-ma a-ta-ma um-ma* DUMU *A-lá-ḫi-im-ma*
6. 10 MA.NA KÙ
7. *ša a-bi$_4$-kà a-ṣa-ba-at*

8. KÙ.BABBAR-*pì i-na ki-ta-im*
9. *za-ru šu-ma šu-ut* 10 MA.NA
10. KÙ.BABBAR *i-ṣa-ba-at a-ta*
11. 11 MA.NA KÙ.BABBAR *ša a-bi*$_4$*-šu*
12. *ṣa-ba-at mì-na-am*
13. *a-na a-bi*$_4$*-šu ḫa-bu-lá-ku-ma*

Edge 14. *ma* KÙ.BABBAR-*pì i-ṣa-ba-at*

Rev. 15. *šu-ma-ma* KÙ.BABBAR *ḫa-bu-lá-⌜ak*$^!$*-⌝šu-um*
16. *ší-bi*$_4$*-šu li-ir-dí-a-ma*
17. *ú-lá ṭup-pu-šu ḫa-ar-ma-am*
18. *lu-ub-lam-ma* KÙ.BABBAR-*áp-šu*
19. *a-na-kam ša-qá-lá-am*
20. *lá a-le-e um-ma a-bu-šu-ma*
21. *gi*$_5$*-im-lá-ni* AN.NA-*kà-am*
22. 1 GÙ *ša ik-ri-bi*$_4$*-<a>*
23. *li-qí-ma* 10 MA.NA KÙ.BABBAR
24. *lá ta-ba-ta-qá-am*
25. 1 GÚ AN.NA *šu-uq-lam*
26. *wa-sú-um-tám li-qí-ma*

Edge 27. *iš-tù u*$_4$*-mì-im*
28. *ša ta-lá-qí-ú*

Left Edge 29. *a-na e-dí-šu* 10 MA.NA KÙ.BABBAR
30. *ṣa-ru-pá-am dí-šu-um*

Translation of Pa. 13 = L 29–567

(1) Thus (says) Asshur-īdī. (3) Speak (2) to Asshur-nādā: (3) Why (4) did you write me (5) saying (lit., you said), The son of Al(i)-aḫum is saying, (7) I will seize (6) the 10 manas of silver (7) of your father? (8) My silver (9) has been squandered (8) in linen. (9) If he (10) really seizes (9) 10 manas of (10) silver, you yourself (12) seize (11) 11 manas of silver belonging to his father! (12) What (13) do I owe to his father? (14) Why does he seize my silver? (15) If I really owe silver to him, (16) let him bring forth his witnesses (17) or (18) let him bring (17) his encased tablet, (18) since (20) I am not able (19) to weigh out (18) his silver (19) here.

(20) Thus his father (said): (21) Do me a favor! (23) Take (22) one talent (of) (21) tin (22) belonging to my *ikribū*-funds (23) and (24) do not sell cheaper than (23) 10 manas of silver. (26) Take (25) one talent of tin,

(26) a fair (25) load, (26) and (27) from the day (28) that you take (it), (30) give to him (29) only the 10 manas of (30) refined (29) silver.

Notes on Pa. 13 = 29–567

Line 5— For the PN Al(i)-aḫum, see Pa. 5:2 above.

Line 6— Note the abbreviated spelling KÙ for KÙ.BABBAR.

Line 8— *Ki-ta-im* is to be understood as *kitûm* (*kitā'um*), "flax, linen"; see Veenhof AOATT 146f., notes 252f., and especially pages 151f. where our text must now be added.

Line 9— I understand *za-ru* as a G stative of *zarā'um*. No other occurrences of this verb in OA are known to me.

Line 14— *Mā* in the sense of "why, how so, what?" is treated in GKT Section 106d. The *ma* is more normal looking on the tablet than Mrs. Lewy drew it.

Line 16— For this use of *radā'um*, see AHw 965a.

Line 17— *Ṭup-pu-šu* = *ṭuppašu* by vowel harmony.

Lines 21-24— These lines are treated by Veenhof AOATT 402. For *ikribū*, see Pa. 7:9 above. The expected *a* at the end of *ik-ri-*bi_4 is missing on the tablet.

The *ba* (line 24) of *tabattaqam* is poorly written.

Lines 25f.— The expression *šuqlam wasumtam* is treated by Veenhof AOATT 15 and 29, n. 57.

Line 30— *Dí-šu-um* = *dinšum*.

Pa. 14 = L 29–568

1. *um-ma A-šùr-i-dí-ma*
2. *a-na A-šùr-na-da qí-*[*bi-m*]*a*
3. *a-šu-mì* KÙ.BABBAR *ša* ⸢*Kà-*⸣*ri-a*
4. *ù ku-a-tí* / *ša tù-šé-bi-lá-ni*
5. *um-ma* ⸢*ša*⸣ *ki-ma* / *Kàr-ri-a-ma*
6. *lu-qú-tám a-na i-ta-aṭ-li-im-ma*
7. *li-dí-in-ma* KÙ.BABBAR
8. *lu-šé-bi-*⸢*lam*⸣ / *la ú-wa-šar*
9. *a-pu-tum a-na i-ta-aṭ-li-*⸢*im*⸣
10. *lu-qú-tám* / *dì-in-ma*
11. *mì-iš-li-šu* KÙ.BABBAR *šé-bi-lam*

12. *ú-ṣa-*<*u-*>*kà* / *la i-ba-ší*
13. KÙ.BABBAR-*ap a-wi-lim a-na na-ru-qí-im*
14. *mì-ma* / *la ta-na-ší*
15. *ù šu-ma* / *i-qí-šu-ni*
16. *mì-ma* / *la ta-lá-qí*
Edge 17. *šu-ma* / *Kà-ri-a*
18. *i-na* KÙ.BABBAR / *a-dí-im*
Rev. 19. *me-ra-šu* / *i-na ša-ḫa-tí-kà*
20. *li-zi-*⌜*iz-*⌝*ma*
21. *ṭup-pá-am ša ší-a-ma-tim*
22. *ší-ta-me-a-ma* / *ší-ma-am*
23. *dí-na-ma* KÙ.BABBAR *mì-iš-li-šu*
24. *ku-un-kà-ma*
25. *šé-bi-lá-nim ki-ma*
26. *ú-ra-am a-na ma-mì-tim*
27. *la i-ṣa-bu-tù-kà-ni*
28. KÙ.BABBAR *i-na šé-bu-lim*
29. *ší-bi šu-ku-un*
30. *šu-ma um-ma me-ra-šu-ma*
31. *lu-qú-tám* / *dí-nam a-na*
32. *a-wa-at* É *a-bi-a*
33. *ma-aṣ-a-ku* / *ma-a*
34. *i-na a-wa-tim ip-tù-a-kà*
35. *um-ma a-ta-ma* / *ma-lá*
36. *i-na* É *a-bi-kà*
Edge 37. *i-ṣé-ri-a i-lá-qí-ú-ni*
38. *i-na ṣé-ri-kà*
Left Edge 39. *a-lá-qí* / *ṭup-pá-kà ù ší-bi-kà*
40. *da-ni-in* / *lu-qú-tám wa-šé-er*

Translation of Pa. 14 = L 29–568

(1) Thus (says) Asshur-īdī. (2) To Asshur-nādā speak. (3) In regard to Karria's (4) and your (3) silver (4) which you sent to me, (5) Karria's representative said, (7) Let him sell (6) the goods for cash (7) and (8) let him send (7) the silver (8) to me. He will not turn (it) loose! (9) Pay attention! (10) Sell the merchandise (9) for cash (10) and (11) send me half the silver! (12) You must not go out on business ventures! (14) You must not take up (13) a man's silver for a sack (14) at all! (15) And even

if they give (you) something as a gift, (16) you must not take anything at all! (17) If Karria (18) has a share in the silver, (20) let (19) his son (20) stand (19) at your side (20) and (22) pay strict attention to (21) the tablet listing the purchases (22) and (23) sell (them) and (24) seal (23) half the silver (24) and (25) send (it) to me. (29) Establish witnesses (28) of the shipping (of) the silver (25) so that (27) he may not prosecute (lit., seize for oath) you (26) some day.

(30) If his son (should say): (31) Give me the goods. (33) I agree (31) with (32) the word of my father's house. (33) Why (34) has he opened up the matter with you? (35) then you (shall say), Whatever (37) he should take (36) in your father's house (37) from my account, (39) I shall take (38) from your account.

(40) Validate (39) your tablet and your witnesses! (40) Release the merchandise!

Notes on Pa. 14 = L 29–568

Line 5— *Kàr* is sure after collation.

Lines 6 and 9— *Ana itaṭlim nadānum* = "to sell for cash." See AHw 767b (sub *naṭālum*) and J. Lewy in HUCA 27 (1956) 75, n. 323 and OrNS 29 (1960) 31, n. 6.

Collation shows there is a *ma* at the end of the next line under the *im* following the first occurrence of this idiom.

Line 12— Literally, "your going out does not exist." *Ú-ṣa-kà* must be taken as a G infinitive with the possessive pronoun *ka*. Usually the infinitive of this verb includes the proper case ending; we have, therefore, interpolated *u*.

Line 18— *A-dí-im* is a G stative of the verb *adāmum*, "to own a share in a common fund," CAD A_1 95f.; "to procure," AHw 10a.

Lines 19f.— *Ina šaḫātika lizziz* means something like "let him serve as your surety" or "let him share the responsibility of the debt." J. Lewy in JAOS 58 (1938) 457, n. 25 and ZA NF 37 (1926/27) 132f. saw *šaḫātum* as an infinitive of the verbal root meaning "to take action." See now, however, OACP 37 and ATHE 26.

The *iz* of line 20 is a little damaged on the top left but is clearly the scribe's intention.

Lines 21–23 are rendered by Veenhof AOATT 388, while lines 21–25a are translated on page 369.

Line 22— *Ší-ta-me-a-ma* is a Gtn imperative of *šamā'um*. See GKT Section 95f.

Line 24— The *ku* at the beginning of the line is intact.

Line 25— *Kīma* here means "that, so that"; see GKT Section 154e.

Line 29— *Šībī šukun* ("establish witnesses!") means to have a particular transaction witnessed and recorded for reference in case of future legal action.

Line 33— For *mā* as an expression of surprise or opposition, see GKT Section 106d.

The scribe is careful to distinguish the *ku*  from the *ma* 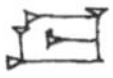 throughout.

Pa. 15 = L 29–569

1. *um-ma Ḫi-na-a* ⌜*ša*⌝ *ki-ma ku-a-tí*
2. *ù Púzur-A-šùr a-na Pu-šu-ki-in*
3. *qí-bi-ma* 28 1/3 MA.NA KÙ.BABBAR
4. *ú* 1 2/3 MA.NA KÙ.GI DINGIR-*ma-lik*
5. *ub-lam*! 6 5/6 GÍN TA KÙ.BABBAR-≪*pì*-≫*ap-šu*
6. 11 1/3 MA.NA 3 GÍN ŠU.NIGÍN 39 5/6? MA.NA
7. KÙ.BABBAR-*ap-kà* ŠÀ.BA 4 GÚ 20 MA.NA 3 1/3 GÍN
8. AN.NA *ku-nu-ku* 40 MA.NA AN.NA *qá-tim*
9. 16 GÍN TA *ú* 6 GÍN KÙ.BABBAR
10. *ni-ik-bu-us* KÙ.BABBAR-*áp-šu*
11. 18 5/6 MA.NA 1 GÍN 1 *me-at* 10 *ku-ta-nu*
12. *ša qá-tim qá-dum ša li-wi-tim*
13. 8 ^{túg}*ku-ta-nu* SIG$_5$ 2 ^{túg}
14. *kà-am-sú-tum* 11 1/2 MA.NA 2/3 GÍN

Edge 15. KÙ.BABBAR *it-bu-lu* 6 ANŠE

16. *ṣa-lá-mu* 2 MA.NA KÙ.BABBAR

Rev. 17. *ší-im-šu-nu* 13 GÍN *ú-nu-sú-nu*

18. 3 GÍN *ú-ku-ul-ta-šu-nu*
19. 4 1/2 GÍN *ša sá-i-tim*
20. 15 GÍN KÙ.BABBAR DINGIR-*ma-lik il*$_5$-*qí*
21. *um-ma šu-ut-ma da-a-at*
22. *ṣú-ḫa-ri* 1/3 MA.NA 1 GÍN
23. KÙ.BABBAR *lu i-na sà-ú-tim*
24. *lu i-na i-ší-ra-tim*
25. *im-ṭí* 2 MA.NA KÙ.BABBAR *a-na*
26. *ḫu-bu-li-kà a-na Im-dí-lim*
27. *ni-dí-in mì-ma a-nim*
28. DINGIR-*ma-lik i-ra-dí-a-kum*

29. *ši-tí* KÙ.BABBAR-*pí-kà* 4 1/3 MA.NA 5 GÍN
30. 26 ^{túg}*ku-ta-nu* 2 MA.NA KÙ.BABBAR
31. *it-bu-lu* 1 ANŠE 1/3 MA.NA 1 1/2 GÍN
32. *ši-im-šu* 5 MA.NA AN.NA *qá-tim*
33. 1/3 MA.NA KÙ.BABBAR-*ap-šu*
34. 2 1/2 GÍN KÙ.BABBAR *ú-nu-ut* ANŠE
35. 18 GÍN *wa-ṣí-tum*

Left Edge 36. 1/3 MA.NA 3 GÍN KÙ.BABBAR *a-na* ANŠE *ni-iš-qú-ul*
37. *me-et* 15 MA.NA AN.NA *ku-nu-ki-ni mì-ma a-nim*
38. ^{d}UTU-*ba-ni i-ra-dí-a-kum* KÙ.BABBAR *ša šé-ep* DINGIR-*ma-*⌜*lik*⌝
39. *gam-ra-kum*

Translation of Pa. 15 = L 29–569

(1) Thus (say) Ḫinnā, your representative, (2) and Puzur-Asshur: to Pūshu-kēn (3) speak. (4) Ilī-malik (5) has brought to me (3) 28 1/3 manas of silver (4) and 1 2/3 manas of gold. (5) At a rate of 6 5/6 shekels (of silver per one shekel of gold), its silver (equivalent is) (6) 11 1/3 manas (and) 3 shekels (to make a) total of 39 2/3(!) manas (as) (7) your silver. From (this amount) 4 talents, 20 manas, (and) 3 1/3 shekels (8) of tin (bearing) seals (were purchased, as well as) 40 manas of average-quality tin (9) at the rate of 16 shekels (of tin) per (shekel of silver); and (10) we paid a gratuity of (9) 6 shekels of silver—(its) equivalent in silver (is) 18 5/6 manas (and) one shekel. (11) 110 (12) average-quality (11) cloths (12) together with coverings, (13) 8 good-quality cloths (and) 2 *kamsum*-textiles (15) brought (14) 11 1/2 manas (and) 2/3 of a shekel of (15) silver. (17) The cost of (15) 6 (16) black (15) donkeys (was) (16) 2 manas of silver; (17) their harness (cost) 13 shekels; (18) their food (cost) 3 shekels (19) (and) the *sa'utum*-fund (was) 4 1/2 shekels. (20) Ilī-malik took 15 shekels of silver.

(21) Thus he (said): (22) The lads' (21) road-fee (of) (22) 1/3 of a mana (and) 1 shekel of (23) silver (25) was deducted (23) either from the *sa'utum*-fund (24) or from the "normal(?)"-fund. (27) We gave (25) 2 manas of silver for (26) your debt to Imdīlum. (28) Ilī-malik will bring (27) all this (28) to you. (29) The rest of your silver (amounts to) 4 1/3 manas (and) 5 shekels. (30) 26 cloths (31) brought (30) 2 manas of silver. (32) The price (of) (31) one donkey (was) 1/3 of a mana (and) 1 1/2

shekels. (32) 5 manas of average-quality tin (33) (cost) 1/3 of a mana (of) silver; (34) the donkey's harness (cost) 2 1/2 shekels of silver. (35) The exit tax (was) 18 shekels. (36) We weighed out the 1/3 of a mana (and) 3 shekels of silver for the donkey. (37) (It is) dead—15 manas of tin (bearing) our seals—(38) Shamash-bāni will bring to you (37) all this. (38) The silver of Ilī-malik's caravan (39) has been spent for you.

Notes on Pa. 15 = L 29-569

Lines 1–18 are treated by H. Lewy in RSO 39 (1964) 184f.

Line 5— *Ub-lam* for *ūbilam*, see GKT Section 93c.

Line 6— The number should be 39 2/3, but the tablet has 39 5/6 though squeezed.

Line 7— The vertical wedges of ŠÀ are on the text, though faint.

Line 8— *Ša qātim* (literally, "of the hand") was taken by H. Lewy as "loose" (RSO 39 [1964] 184). Veenhof (AOATT 199–201), however, has argued convincingly for "of normal, current quality." We have the expression without *ša* here and in line 32. The full form appears in line 12.

Line 10— For the verb *kabāsum* and its substantive, *kibsum*, see H. Lewy's comments in RSO 39 (1964) 184, n. 4; CAD K 339a (sub *kibsu*); GKT Section 8b (and n. 2) and AHw 472a.

Line 11— For *kutānum*, see the note on Pa. 3:4.

Line 14— For ^{túg}*kà-am-sú-tum*, a kind of cloth, see CAD K 126b. Add our text to those referred to by Veenhof in AOATT 184.

Line 18— For *ukultum*, "food, provisions, fodder," see GKT Section 63f where TC 3, 18:23; 24:24; and CCT 1, 30a:5 are cited. Add to these references the following: KTH 18:30; ATHE 37:46; KUG 38:24; KTK 27: x + 6; ICK 1, 32:25; BIN 6, 124:15; and an unpublished letter in the Rosenberg collection, lines 32f. (partially transliterated by J. Lewy HUCA 27 [1956] 68, n. 289). These texts show that *ukultum* may designate food for donkeys (TC 3, 18:23; CCT 1, 30a:5; and ATHE 37:46) as well as for persons (ICK 1, 32:25 and BIN 6, 124:15). Special attention should be paid to the Rosenberg letter where the term is used once of food for a donkey and once of a person's food. The other citations are unclear on this issue.

Lines 19 and 23— For *sá-i-tim*, see AHw 999a ("a delivery or payment"). Add to von Soden's list of occurrences, Gelb 58:36 as restored by J. Lewy HUCA 27 (1956) 32, n. 113. See also Larsen OACP 42f. and 152, where Larsen takes Garelli's suggestion that *sa'edim / sa'udum* designated "un objet matériel faisant partie du harnachement" (AC 194f.) as "possible" since the term is never used when metals only are involved. Our text, however, seems to involve the shipment of tin as well as textiles. Lines 21–25 suggest that *sa'utum* either designates a fund or container from which the toll could be paid.

The *sá*, though not perfect, has all its elements .

Line 21— See Larsen OACP 130, 139f., and 169f. for a discussion of *dātum*. Also helpful is J. Lewy's older treatment in HUCA 27 (1956) 45 and 67–69. Of course, Veenhof devoted Part Three of AOATT to his systematic treatment of *dātum* (pages 219–302).

Line 24— *i-ší-ra-tim*. AHw 394b lists a comparable form from ICK 1, 171:3 as well as a singular form (*i-šé-er*$^{!}$*-tim*) from EL 116:4 (VAT 9274) with the questionable meaning of "a normal quantity." CAD E 368b shows the usual plural of *ešrētu*, "tithe," for OA as *išrātum*. Larsen OACP 116, in discussing TC 2, 14:22f. where the exact wording of our text (lines 24f.) appears, rejects the renderings of Van der Meer and Garelli as "tithe" and favors von Soden's rendering, "normal amounts," which is equal to the normal tax paid when the caravan reached Asshur, that is, the *nisḫatu*-tax.

Line 30— The KÙ is dulled but still visible.

Lines 32f.— Note the ratio of 15 to 1 for tin to silver.

Line 35— For *waṣītum* as an exit tax or "export-duty," see Larsen OACP 43 and 152.

Line 37— "(It is) dead" may mean the donkey died or the transaction is finished.

Line 39— For the expression *kaspum gamrakum*, see CAD G 26b.

Pa. 16 = L 29–571

1. *a-na A-mur-Ištar qí-bi-ma*
2. *um-ma Im-dì*-DINGIR-*ma*
3. *ta-ša-pá-ra-am i-ṭup-pì-kà*
4. *um-ma a-ta-ma a-dí* [[x]]
5. *iš-tù Bu-ur-*<*uš-*>*ḫa-tim*
6. *a-la-kà-ni* / *A-šur*-SIG$_5$
7. *a-na a-lim*^{ki} *la ta-*⸢*ṭá-*⸣*ra-ad*

8. *a-la-kam-ma* KÙ.BABBAR 1 MA.NA
9. *ù* 2 MA.NA *iš-tí*
10. *a-ḫi ib-ri / a-be-a-lim*
11. *e-ri-šu-um ù a-na-ku a-da-šu-um*
12. *a-na-ku a-li-bi*$_4$*-kà lá lá-ma-nim*
13. *ak-lá-šu um-ma a-na-ku-ma*
14. *la iš-ta-na-kà-ak a-dí*
15. *i-lá-kà-ni eq-lu-um*
Edge 16. *lu-kà-i-il*$_5$*-šu / a-ta*
17. *ta-ra-kà-ba-am*
Rev. 18. *a-na Tí-iš-mu-ur-na*
19. *um-ma a-ta-ma*
20. *ša-ni-ú-tum*$_8$ É *a-bi*$_4$*-ni*
21. *i-ta-bu-lu ù i-a-tí*
22. *ad-ma-ni mì-na-am*
23. *ḫa-bu-la-ku ša mì-ma*
24. *la ta-lá-qí-ú / a-na* KÙ.BABBAR*-pì-a*
25. *ta-áš-ta-na-kà-an*
26. *ù iš-tù u*$_4$*-ri-im ku*$^!$*-wa-tí*
27. *lu ḫa-⸢bu-⸣lá-ku qá-té-e*
28. *a-ḫe-e-ma ù a-ta*
29. *la ta-ša-ḫu-ut šu-ma-⸢me-en⸣*
30. *ki-ma a-na-kam ḫa-bu-lu*
31. *ù a-ma-kam sí-ku-šu ú-kà-il*$_5$
32. *la me-en tù-ša-ḫi-it*
Edge 33. *um-ma-me-en a-ta-ma*
34. *lá <u->kà-i-lá-šu a-wa-at a-lim*^{ki}
Left Edge 35. *la tí-dé-e / ša eq-lim / i-na*
36. *eq-lim-ma i-lá-qí ša a-lim*^{ki}
37. *i-na a-lim*^{ki}*-ma i-lá-qí*

Translation of Pa. 16 = L 29–571

(1) Say to Amur-Ishtar: (2) Thus (says) Imdi-ilum: (3) You are writing me. In your tablet (4) you say: Until (6) I come (5) from Burushḫaddum, (7) do not send (6) Asshur-damiq (7) to the City (of Assur). (8) I will go and (11) I will request for him (8) one (9) or two manas (of) (8) silver (10) for investment (9) with (10) a brother, a partner.

(11) Furthermore I myself will give (it) to him. (12) I myself (13) have held him back (12) so as not to make your heart feel bad.

(13) Thus I said: (14) He must not continually "tear (things) up"! Until (15) he comes, (16) let (15) the Province (16) hold him back! You yourself (17) should ride here.

(18) At Tishmurna (19) you (said): (20) Others (21) are carrying away (20) our father's house! (21) But (22) hold shares in a common fund (21) for me. (22) What (23) do I owe? Whatever (24) you fail to take (25) you may continually deposit (24) to my silver (account). (26) So after tomorrow (27) I will (indeed) owe (it) (26) to you (as if to) (27) the hand of (28) a foreigner. But you (29) should not fear. If (30) he had owed (anything) here (31) and had seized his (garment's) hem there, (32) you would not have intimidated (him). (33) If you were to say, (34) "I did not hold him!" (35) you do not understand (34) the order of the City (of Assur), (36) (namely), one should buy (35) (the goods) of the Province in (36) the Province. (But) (37) one must buy (36) (the goods) of the City (of Assur) (37) in the City (of Assur).

Notes on Pa. 16 = L 29–571

Line 1— The *mur* is perfectly clear on the text.

Line 4— There is an erased sign at the end of the line, probably an *iš*.

Line 5— Collation shows that H. Lewy's drawing is correct. Although we have restored the well known GN Burušḫaddum, Burḫaddum might be retained as a rare GN on the strength of CCT 6, 37a:3 and 9 (*Bu-ur-ḫa-tim*).

Line 7— The traces may suggest TA or ŠA with the context favoring TA = *ṭá*. For the verb *ṭarādum*, "to dispatch, send on a mission," see GKT Section 78d.

Line 11— *E-ri-šu-um* may be understood variously, either as a PN, a G imperative, or as a G present. The context demands a verb rather than the well known PN. The verb *erāšum* is discussed in GKT Section 90. Following *allakamma* in line 8, we expect a G present. *Ēriššum* may be understood as a present form, in spite of the fact that such verbs usually take an "a" as the second vowel in the present and that the normal preterite is *eriš* (< *irriš*). See TTC 27:5–10: (5) . . . *a-*[*ḫu-kà*] (6) *a-na Bu-ru-uš-ḫa-tim* (7) *a-ṣé-er ru-ba-im* GAL (8) *i-ša-pár-šu-ma* / *iš-tí* (9) *kà-ri-im e-na-na-tim* (10) *e-ri-iš-ma*. . . . The context demands that the verb in line 10 be taken as a present, "he will ask."

See CAD E 281ff. (especially 281b) for the present of this root in *ēriš*. Other examples of the present form of *erāšum* are: EL 180:9 (*té-ri-šu*) (= KTH 23) and possibly Garelli, MAH 19614 (RA 60 [1966] 109f.):19.

Line 14— *Iš-ta-na-kà-ak* as a Gtn of ŠKK, ŠGG, ŠQQ is most difficult. So far as I know, such a verb appears nowhere else in OA. The modern dictionaries are little help. AHw 1134 recognizes a root *šakākum*, "to put in a row, to harrow," in the G and D stems. No Gtn is listed. The context suggests some troublesome action or negative feeling since the next statement is a wish that the enigmatic "he" should be delayed on his journey.

Line 18— *Ana Tišmurna* perhaps should be read with line 17 as an afterthought after the verb, *tarakkabam*, had already been written.

Lines 20f. are rendered by Veenhof in AOATT 441 sub g.

Lines 24f.— *Ana kaspia taštanakan*. Veenhof AOATT 432–438 treats the verb *šakānum* in its various idioms, especially in the expression *šakānum ana. . . .* The usual meaning of "to deposit to" fits our case very well in the sense of "to add to." The idiom of our text should be added to Veenhof's discussion since he notes no text either a) using the Gtn form or b) making *kaspim* the object of *ana*. Obviously our *ana kaspia* is equivalent to Veenhof's *ana nikkassī*. The use of the Gtn seems to have no particularly specialized significance beyond the normal iterative sense.

Line 26— The collation of this line is reflected in our transliteration. The *ku-wa-tí* is squeezed at the end of the line so that the *wa* was begun on top of the last vertical wedge of the *ku*. Only the head of the vertical wedge remains barely visible.

See GKT Section 48b for *ku-wa-tí* as the dative form of *ku-a-tí*, "you" in the singular.

I can find no other examples of *ištu urrim*, "from the day, after tomorrow." "From (that) day" is also possible; but since *urram* occurs occasionally in the sense of "tomorrow," we have preferred "after tomorrow."

Lines 27f.— *Qá-té-e a-ḫe-e-ma*. *Qá-té-e* must be taken as the singular construct of *qātum*, "hand." *A-ḫe-e-ma* could be taken from *aḫum*, "brother," or *aḫû*, "stranger, alien, outsider." The scribe's care in writing the long vowel suggests the latter possibility.

Line 29— *Tašaḫḫut* is a normal G present of *šaḫātum*, "to be frightened, fear." The D present of this root appears in line 32 (*tušaḫḫit*) in the sense of "to produce fear, intimidate."

Lines 29, 32, and 33— The enclitic *me-en* to designate contrary-to-fact statements is discussed in GKT Sections 106e and 139.

Line 31— "To hold the hem of someone's garment" means to force that one legally to make good on an obligation. See J. Lewy OrNS 29 (1960) 21 (also n. 3) and AHw 1042. See also J. Lewy's older discussion of the hem of the garment in RHR 110 (1934) 31–33.

Line 34— *Lá kà-i-lá-šu* is problematic. The verbal form appears to be a D imperative, but the imperative may not be negated by any of the three negative particles (GAG Section 81a). The form would have to be written *lu-kà-i-lá-šu* if the D precative were intended. If the scribe intended to write a negative command by means of *lā* prefixed to the stative, he should have written *lá kà-ú-lá-šu*, although I know of no examples of the D stative of this verb. Another possibility must be considered, namely, to interpolate *ú* before the verb with the meaning "I did not seize him." We have followed the latter suggestion as it makes reasonable sense in the context.

Pa. 17 = L 29–572

1. *um-ma A-lá-ḫu-um-ma*
2. *a-na A-šùr-na-da*
3. *qí-bi*$_4$*-ma* 1/3 MA.NA KÙ.GI
4. *ša Púzur-A-na*
5. *iš-qú-lá-ni i-na*
6. *Ḫa-ḫi-im* É.GAL-*lúm*
7. *iṣ-ru-up-šu-ma a-na*
8. KÙ.BABBAR-*pì-ma i-tù-ar*
9. *ù* 5 *u*$_4$*-me ú-ša-as-ḫi-ri*
10. *ù* 10 GÍN KÙ.BABBAR
11. *ra-ag-ma-am*
12. *i-na ṣé-ri-a*

Edge 13. *el-tí-qí / a-na Kà-ni-ìš*
14. *a-ta-ú-ri-im*

Rev. 15. *a-zi-iz-ma um-ma*
16. *a-na-*⸢*ku-*⸣*ma ki-i-na* <*i-na*>
17. *kà-ri-im Kà-ni-iš*
18. *pu-ru-šu lá áš-ku-un*
19. *a-ší-a-tí lá ú-ta-i-ra-šu*
20. *a-pu-tum a-pu-tum*
21. KÙ.GI *ša i-ša-qá-lá-ku-ni*
22. *a-na i-ša-tim*

23. *ší-ni-šu ta-ir-šu*
24. *a-na* KÙ.BABBAR *ša A-šùr-be-el-a-wa-tim*
25. *i-ḫi-id-ma* KÙ.BABBAR
26. *lá i-ru-aq a-na*
27. *Tí-mì-il$_5$-ki-<a> is-li-i-ma*
28. *lá i-tal-kam*
29. DINGIR *lu i-dí*
30. KÙ.BABBAR *ma-lá i-na ba-áb-tí-a*
31. *ta-ma-ḫu-ru a-na ≪a-na≫ a-lim*
32. *šé-bi$_4$-lam ší-mu i-ba-ší*

Translation of Pa. 17 = L 29–572

(1) Thus (says) Al(i)-aḫum: (3) Speak (2) to Asshur-nādā. (6) The Palace (5) in (6) Ḫaḫḫum (7) smelted (3) the 1/3 of a mana of gold (7) for him (i.e., Puzur-Ana) (4) which Puzur-Ana (5) weighed out for me, (7) and (8) it (the gold) will come back (7) as (8) silver. (9) It held me back 5 days! (13) Consequently it took (10) 10 shekels of silver (11) (as) a claim (12) against my account. (15) I took my stand (14) for returning (it) (13) to Kanish (15) and (so) thus (16) I (said): Truly in (17) the Mercantile Center (*kārum*) of Kanish (18) I did not slander him! (19) I did not send him back to that (place, i.e., Ḫaḫḫum).

(20) Pay close attention! (23) Return (21) the gold which he will weigh out to you (23) a second time (22) to the (smelting) fire. (25) Watch over (24) Asshur-bēl-awātum's silver (25) so that the silver (26) should not get away. At (27) Timilkia he kept me in ignorance and (28) did not come here. (29) The god certainly knows (the truth of the matter)! (32) Send (30) whatever silver (31) you receive (30) from my merchandise (31) to the City (of Assur where) (32) purchases are (possible).

Notes on Pa. 17 = L 29–572

Line 1— See Pa. 5:2 above for the PN Al(i)-aḫum.

Lines 7f.— See Veenhof AOATT 351 and 365 for the thrust of *ana* KÙ.BABBAR *tu'ārum* (G). The implied subject of the verb *itu''ar* might be Puzur-Ana, however, with the meaning that Puzur-Ana will return later for the silver.

Line 9— The verb *ú-ša-*AZ*-ḫi-ri* must derive from the root *saḫārum*, "to stop, hold back," since no Š stem is attested for the verb, *ṣaḫārum*, "to be small, deduct." See AHw 1007b.

Line 11— The adjective *ragmum* in the expression *kaspam ragmum* is unknown to me elsewhere. For the verb *ragāmum*, see AHw 941b and GKT Sections 88a, b, and 125d.

Lines 12f.— For the idiom *ina ṣēr . . . laqā'um*, "to charge interest against, to debit," see CAD Ṣ 140b.

Line 16— For *kī* as a preposition with the same uses as *kīma*, see GKT Section 103f; used as a conjunction, GKT page 181, n. 1. We prefer to take KI I NA as a scribal error for *ki-i-na* <*i-na*> by haplography. The verbal form is ambiguous. We have followed the most straightforward rendering in our translation. But the verb might be dealt with as a precative: "Let me firmly establish his slander in the Kanish Mercantile Center!"

Line 18— For *pu-ru-šu*, "vulgarity, slander," see AHw 882a; used with the verb *šakānum* in the sense of "to bring abuse upon someone," AHw 1136b. *Pu-ra-šu* is expected as the accusative but has changed by vowel harmony.

Line 31— Collation shows that the extra *ana* is on the tablet.

Line 32— The expression *šīmū ibašši* is thus rendered by Veenhof AOATT 377.

Pa. 18 A = L 29–573 Inner Tablet

1. *um-ma wa-ak-lúm-ma*
2. *a-na Pu-šu-ki-in*
3. *qí-bi-ma* / *a-na-kam-ma*
4. *a-bi* / *ú-na-ḫi-id-kà*
5. *um-ma šu-ut-ma* / *šu-ma me-er-i a-ta*
6. *šu-ma ta-ra-a-ma-ni*
7. KÙ.BABBAR-*áp* / *Ás-qú-dim*
8. *ṣa-ba-at* / *a-ni i-na ṭup-pì-kà*
9. *ta-áš-pu-ra-am*
10. *um-ma a-ta-ma* / *a-wi-lúm*
11. *i-na qá-qí-ri-im*
12. *da-nim* / *wa-ša-áb*
13. [*lá e-*]*ta-lá-ku-ma*!

Edge 14. [KÙ.]BABBAR *lá a-ṣa-ba-at*

Rev. 15. *šu-ma a-bi*$_4$ *a-ta*

16. *šu-ma ta-ra-a-ma-ni*
17. *a-ma* 2 *ṭup-pè-en*
18. *na-áš-ú-ni-ku-um*
19. *iš-tí-in* / *ṭup-pá-am šé-me*
20. 1 *ṭup-pá-am* / *i-na qá-tí-kà*
21. *kà-i-il*$_5$ / *šu-ma a-bi*$_4$ *a-ta*
22. *šu-ma ta-ra-a-ma-ni*
23. *a-bu-ni lu-qú-tám ma-a-tám*
24. *i-dí-šu-um lu e-ta-lá-tí-ṃa*
25. *iš-tù* KÙ.BABBAR 1 GÚ *ù e-li-iš*
26. *ṣa-ba-at* / KÙ.BABBAR 1 GÍN
27. *lá i-ḫa-li-iq ki-ma*
28. *ša a-ta* / *ta-qí-ša-ni*
29. *li-bi*$_4$ *ḫa-dí* IGI *A-šur*

Edge 30. *ù i-li-a a-kà-ra-ba-kum*$^!$

31. ⌜*ki-*⌝*ma* KÙ.BABBAR-*áp ra-mì-ni-kà*
32. *šu-tám-ri-iṣ*

Left Edge 33. *a-šu-mì a-wa-tí-kà* / *ša i-bu-lu*$^!$*-uṭ a-bi*$_4$*-a*

34. *ta-áp-tí-a-ni ù ṭup-pá-kà*$^!$ / *áš-*⌜*ta-me*⌝
35. *a-na-ku a-na-kam ma-ṣa-ku-um*

Pa. 18 B = L 29–573 Case

1. [KIŠIB *wa-ak-*]*lim*
2. [*a-na P*]*u-šu-ki-in* DUMU ZU-*e-a*
3. [*a-na a-*]*wa-at ṭup-pì-im*
4. [*i-ḫ*]*i-id ù ṭup-pá-am*
5. [*ša*] *A-mur-Ištar* DUMU *A-mur-*DINGIR
6. [*na-*]*áš-ú* / *ṭup-pá-am*
7. [*l*]*e-qé-ma* / *šé-bi*$_4$*-lam*
8. *a-ta ki-ma ta-le-e-ú*
9. *e-pu-uš* / ŠA KU KAM
10. *a-na qá-áb-li-kà*
11. *na-áš-ú-ni-kum*

Edge 12. *ṭup-pá-am iš-tí-in*

13. *pè-té-ma* / *ší-ta-me*
14. [1] *ṭup-pá-am kà-i-il*$_5$

Rev. 15. *a-na pì-am lu ma-al-a-tí-ma*

16. *lu*$^!$ *e-ta-lá-tí*

Seal Inscription

1. [ ]x
2. [PA.TE.]SI
3. [^{d}*A-*]*šùr*
4. DUMU *I-ku-*[ ]
5. ENSÍ
6. ^{d}*A-šùr*

Translation of Pa. 18 A = L 29–573 Inner Tablet

(1) Thus (says) the City Ruler (*waklum*): (3) Speak (2) to Pūshukēn. Here (4) my father instructed you (5) saying: If you are my son, (6) if you love me, (8) seize (7) Asqudum's silver!

(8) Now (9) you have written to me (8) in your tablet (10) saying: The man (12) is residing (11) in a (12) dangerous (11) place; (13) so I am not going up (to deal with him) for you. (14) I am not seizing the silver.

(15) If you are my father, (16) if you love me,—(17) behold (18) they are carrying to you (17) two tablets. (19) Listen to one tablet; (21) hold (20) one tablet in your hand! (21) If you are my father, (22) if you love me,—(23) our father (24) gave to him (i.e., Asqudum) (23) much merchandise. (24) You must act bravely and (26) seize (25) at least one talent of silver. (27) Not (26) a single shekel of silver (27) should be lost! As if (28) you were giving (it) to me as a present, (29) make my heart happy! (Then) before Asshur (20) and my god I will pray for you. (32) Exert yourself (in this matter) (31) as if (it were) your own silver!

(33) In regard to your matter which (34) you opened up (33) during my father's lifetime (34) and (about which) I had listened (in) your tablet, (35) here I am intervening for you.

Translation of Pa. 18 B = L 29–573 Case

(1) [The seal impression of the City] Ruler (*waklum*).(2) [To Pū]shukēn son of Su'en-Ea. (4) [Pay atten]tion (3) [to the ma]tter of the tablet! (4) And as for the tablet (5) which Amur-Ishtar son of Amur-ilī (6) is carrying, (7) take (6) the tablet (7) and send (it) to me! (8) As for you, (9) do (8) as you are able! (11) They are carrying (10) for your waist (9) the . . . (13) Open (12) one tablet (13) and hear (it). (14) Hold [one] tablet. (15) You must fulfill the order and (16) act bravely!

Translation of the Seal Inscription

(1) [PN], (2) [the Gover]nor of (3) Asshur, (4) son of Ikū[num,] (5) the Governor of (6) Asshur.

Notes on Pa. 18 A = L 29–573 Inner Tablet

J. Lewy (JAOS 78 [1958] 99–101) rendered lines 3b–8a, 15–26a, and 33–35 of this text and discussed its implications relating to some of the economic involvements of the early Assyrian kings. See now Larsen's discussion of our text in The Old Assyrian City-State and Its Colonies (hereafter OACC) 134–136. Both Lewy and Larsen read the seal impression as that of Sargon son of Ikūnum in spite of the impression's poor state of preservation.

Line 13— This line is difficult because of damage to the edge of the text. Mrs. Lewy, after collating the text in 1967, concluded that the line should be read *e lá ik-ta-lá-ku-ma*. See GKT Sections 77d, 105a, and GAG Section 81i/j for the use of the negative particle *ē*. My collation, however, favors the reading followed in the transliteration above.

Line 24— For *lū ettalātima*, "be independent!" see AHw 260b.

Line 25— For *ištu . . . eliš*, "at least," see Veenhof AOATT 453, n. 561 and CAD E 97b.

Line 28— This line creates a problem. J. Lewy first read *ta*-PÁ-*ša-ni*; he later thought the questionable sign might be *wa*. H. Lewy, after her 1967 collation, suggested either *wa*, *sá*, or *mur*. The verbs with these readings appear to make no sense. *Pá*! makes a reasonable verbal form, *ta-pá-ša-ni*, from *epāšum*. My collation, however, suggests that we may try KI! = *gi*$_5$, *ki*, or *qí*. *Akāšum*, "to go, send," usually has the vowel "u." Thus *takišanni*, "after you go or send," is ruled out. Another possibility is to read *ta-qí-ša-ni* from *qi'āšum*, "to give, remit," which fits the context well. Larsen favors the latter interpretation.

Lines 33f.— In the expression, *aššūmi awātika ša i-bu-lu-uṭ abia taptianni*, *bu-lu-uṭ* may be taken as a D infinitive construct with the meaning "after the healing of my father."

For *patā'um* used with *awātum* in the sense of "to clear up," see AHw 860a sub 19, where TC 2, 17:24 is cited as an example.

Mrs. Lewy's line drawing shows the sign after *ṭup-pa* to be *am*. My collation, however, shows it to be more like a badly drawn *kà*.

Line 35— I take *ma-ṣa-ku-um* as *maṣākkum*. See GKT Section 72a. The extra *a* which Larsen (OACC n. 94 on p. 136) reads (*ma-ṣa-a-ku-um*) is not on the tablet. For *maṣā'um*, "to intervene," see ATHE 33:51′ (note on p. 49) and J. Lewy EL II 20, n. b.

Notes on Pa. 18 B = L 29–573 Case

Line 1— Collation shows the *lim* is the end of the line.

Line 2— We restore *ana* in the lacuna since according to the Tablet the letter was sent to Pūšu-kēn.

Line 4— The ⌜*ḫi*⌝ is questionable after collation, but still possible.

Line 7— Add the word divider as indicated in our transcription which does not show on Mrs. Lewy's line drawing.

Line 9— The last sign is difficult. The remains are  which suggest *kam*, but what *ša-ku-kam* means is far from clear. BIN 6, 78:24 has *ša-ku-kam* unfortunately in a broken context so that it is no help beyond suggesting that our reading is a little more firm. Larsen (OACC n. 94 on p. 135) does not attach *ša* to the other two signs.

Line 14— The beginning of the line is broken. We have restored DIŠ on the basis of the Tablet. There is sufficient space for DIŠ but not enough for a larger sign.

Lines 15 and 16— The *lu* in both lines is strangely written,  Context demands we read *lu*, however.

Note on the Seal Impression on Pa. 18 B

The *waklum*'s seal was pressed on the case three times. Unfortunately, each time the impression is broken off at the same place as shown in H. Lewy's line drawing. Another impression of the same seal appears on Edinburgh 1909/585 (Sayce, Babylonica 4, 65–69, 77 = EL 327) where the first three lines are intact while the last three are broken off. Larsen (OACC 134) also takes the seal impression as that of Sargon's seal. See J. Lewy's discussion of this seal impression in HUCA 27 (1956) 78, n. 332.

Pa. 19 = L 29–574

1. *um-ma Ša-lim-a-ḫu-um-ma*
2. *a-na La-qí-pí-im ù Pu-šu-ki-in*
3. *qí-bi-ma a-ḫu-ú-a a-tù-nu*

4. AN.NA-ki ù TÚG$^{\text{ḫi.a}}$
5. la i-na-ki-mu a-na
6. u$_4$-me-e / qú-ur-bi-tim
7. 9 GÍN TA ù e-li-iš
8. dì-na ù ša u$_4$-me-e pá-tí-ú-tim
9. ma-lá / ta-da-nim dí-na
10. lu-qú-ti lu ša šé-ep
11. DUMU Ìr-ra-a lu ša Dan-A-šùr
12. ÈR-dí-a-ni lu ša ILLAT-at
13. DUMU Šu-^{d}En-líl AN.NA-ki
Edge 14. ù TÚG$^{\text{ḫi.a}}$ ma-lá / iz-ku-ú-ni-ni
15. tí-ir-ta-ak-nu
Rev. 16. li-li-kam 6 ^{túg}ku-sí-tum
17. 1 ^{túg}ni-ib-ra-ru-um
18. ša šé-ep Dan-A-šùr ù ší-im
19. ANŠE$^{\text{ḫi.a}}$ ma-lá ta-áš-a-ma-ni
20. tí-ir-ta-ak-nu li-li-kam
21. 30 1/3 (or 31 1/3) MA.NA 7 GÍN KÙ.BABBAR
22. [u$_4$-]me-e ša ta-áš-pu-ra-ni
23. [x] MA.NA 10 GÍN KÙ.BABBAR ša me-er-e
24. A-šùr-UTU-ši 5 MA.NA KÙ.BABBAR
25. ša Ḫi-na-a mì-ma a-nim
26. ša-áš-qí-lá-ma i-na
27. pá-nim-ma šé-bi-lá-nim
28. ṭup-pu-um ša ší-ma-at
29. A-šùr-i-mì-tí i-na Ḫu-ra-ma
30. iš-tí Ša-lim-A-šùr DUMU En-um-A-⌜šùr⌝
31. i-ba-ší šu-up-ra-ma ṭup-pá-am
32. lu-ub-lu-ni-ku-nu-tí-ma
Left Edge 33. ṭup-pá-am i-na Kà-nu-e lá-wi-a-ma
34. ⌜da-⌝am-qí-iš a-na DUMU um-me-a-nim
35. [ke-]nim pí-iq-da-ma lu-ub-lam a-na
36. wa-bi$_4$-il$_5$ ṭup-[pì-]im KÙ.BABBAR 1 ⌜GÍN⌝ i-na [KÙ.BABBAR]
37. dí-na-šu-um [ ] ù? ša? [ ]

Translation of Pa. 19 = L 29–574

(1) Thus (says) Shalim-aḫum: (3) Speak (2) to Lā-qēpum and Pūshukēn. (3) You (are) my brothers. (5) They should not store up (4) tin and

textiles. (8) Sell (them) (7) for at least 9 shekels each (5) over (6) a short term. (8) Further (9) sell (8) during an open-ended term (9) whatever there is to sell. (16) Let (15) your instruction (16) come to me (10) (concerning) the merchandise (of) (13) tin (14) and textiles, (10) whether of (11) Irra's son's (10) caravan (11) or of Dan-Asshur's, (12) our two servants, or of (13) Shū-Enlil's son's caravan—(14) whatever they have cleared for us. (20) Let your instruction come (concerning) (16) the 6 *kusītum*-garments (and) (17) 1 *nibrarum*-textile, (18) transported by Dan-Asshur, as well as the price of (19) the donkeys—whatever you may have bought.

(26) Pay out (25) all the following: (21) 30 1/3 (or 31 1/3) manas (and) 7 shekels of silver (22) of the term about which you wrote to me, (23) x manas (and) 10 shekels of silver of the sons of (24) Asshur-shamshī (and) the 5 manas of silver (25) of Ḫinnā, (26) and at the (27) earliest send (the silver) to me!

(28) A tablet recording (lit., of) the stipulation of (29) Asshur-imittī (31) is to be found (29) in Ḫurrama (30) with Shalim-Asshur son of Ennum-Asshur. (31) Write to me and (32) let him carry (31) the tablet (32) to you and (33) wrap up the tablet in Kanue, and (34) kindly (35) entrust (it) (34) to a (35) reliable (34) agent (35) and let him bring (it) to me. (37) Pay (35) to (36) the bearer of the tablet 1 shekel from [the silver]. (The remainder of the line is too damaged to read.)

Notes on Pa. 19 = L 29–574

Line 5— We understand *i-na-ki-mu* to be a G present from NKM. The form might be rendered in the passive; but since no N stem is attested, we prefer the G.

Line 6— u_4*-me-e qurbitim* = "near days," with *qurbitim* derived from *qarbum/qurbum*.

Line 8— u_4*-me-e pá-ti-ú-tim* = "open days," obviously expresses the opposite of *umē qurbitim* in line 6. It means "for a period of time of open-ended duration, long-term."

Line 9— For the use of *mala* with infinitive in the sense of "whatever there is to be . . . ," see GKT Section 127e.

Line 12— ÈR-*dí-a-ni* offers problems. We are taking the expression to mean *wardianni*, "our two slaves," referring to Irra's son and Dan-Asshur. We should expect the dual oblique case in *ī* or *ē* rather than the *ān* of the dual nominative. The *dí* is also troublesome; it appears to function as a phonetic complement following the logogram. Perhaps it is simpler to assume a scribal error and transcribe ÈR-*dí*-≪*a*-≫*ni*.

Line 16— ^{túg}*kusītum* in our text adds another exception to Veenhof's note (AOATT 96, n. 157) that *kusītum*-garments in OA texts never number more than four. For further information on *kusītum*, see Veenhof AOATT 153, 159–162, and 163, n. 277.

Line 17— Veenhof (AOATT 172f.) rejects J. Lewy's explanation for the textile name, *nibrarum*, as being derived from *barārum* on the grounds that one would expect *nabrarum* or *nabrirum*. This objection may not be so formidable in the light of Hecker's discussion of the interchange of "a" and "i" in GKT Sections 8b-d. There is, of course, the possibility that the term should be read *né-eb-ra-ru-um*. At the same time it must be kept in mind that *nibrarum* may have been a foreign word. See also AHw 785b.

Line 25— The PN *Ḫi-na-a* is well attested; see EL 114:2; EL I page 127, n. a (= CCT 2, 27:2); PNC 40b *et passim*.

Lines 33–35 are treated by Veenhof (AOATT 28) who takes *ina* GA-*nu-e* as *ina qanu'e*, "in a reed(?)." See AHw 898. We, however, see the term as a GN, *Kà-nu-e*; see EL 6:19f. (= TC 2, 76) where *Kà-nu-e* alternates with *Kà-nu-a*. This GN is unknown to me elsewhere.

Line 36 has a small lacuna at the end large enough to accommodate two signs. The collation notes of J. Lewy from September 14, 1956, show that he saw *kasp*[*i-ni*] in the lacuna. H. Lewy took no note of this possible reading. What remains may be KÙ. There is enough space for BABBAR but not for an additional *a* or *ni*.

Line 37— Neither J. Lewy nor H. Lewy made a suggestion for the lacunas. There is space for about two signs in each lacuna. Neither Lewy noted the possible *ù ša*.

Pa. 20 = L 29–575

1. *um-ma In-bi-Ištar-ma*
2. *a-na Ṣí-lá-*^{d}IM
3. *qí-bi-ma áš-pu-ra-am*
4. *um-ma a-na-ku-ma*
5. *ší-bé-e ša A-šùr-ma-lik*
6. *ḫi-ri-im-ma* / *a-na*
7. 10 u_4*-me-e* / *a-wa-tum*

8. *li-tù-ra-am* u_4*-me-*[*e*?]
9. *a-na ṣú*!*-ḫa-ri áš-ku-un*! [ ]
10. *a-ta* / *a-dí* u_4*-mì-im*[ ]
11. *ta-ak-ta-lá-šu*[ ]
12. *i-na* ^{d}UTU*-ši na-ás-pá*[*r-tí*]
13. *ta-ša-me-ú ṣú-ḫa-ri*
14. *ma-lá a-ma-kam*

Edge 15. *wa-áš-bu-ni ṭù-ur-*[*dam*]
16. *a ša* [ ]

Rev. 17. *mì-nam a-ma-kam*
18. *wa-áš-bu ù a-ta*
19. *lá ṣú-ba-tí* / *tí-šu ú-lá*
20. *ša-áp-tám* / *tí-šu* / *a-dí* 10 u_4*-me-*[*e*]
21. *ra-ma-kà za-ki-ma*
22. *al-kam-ma a-na Ni-na-ša-a*
23. *a-lik* / *ma-ma-an* / *la-šu*
24. *ša* AN.NA 10 MA.NA
25. *ù* TÚG$^{hi.a}$ 10 / *uš-tí-bu*[ ]
26. *ba-áb-tám* 1 GÍN *lá té-zi-ib* [ ]
27. *lá ta-qá-bi*$_4$ *um-ma a-ta-ma*
28. *ba-áb-tám* / *e-zi-ba-am*
29. KÙ.BABBAR *i-na ba-áb-tim i-a-tim*
30. *ša ta-lá-qí-ú a-ḫa-ma*
31. *i-na ku-nu-ki-šu li-ib-ší*

Edge 32. *a-wa-tum*$_9$ *ša iš-tù*
33. *a-lim*^{ki} *i-ma-qú-tám*
34. *ú na-áš-pè-er-tám*

Left Edge 35. *ša a-bi*$_4$*-ni pá-ni-tám-ma šu-up-ra-am*

Translation of Pa. 20 = L 29–575

(1) Thus (says) Inbi-Ishtar: (3) Speak (2) to Ṣilla-Adad. I wrote (4) saying: (Write the names of) (5) Asshur-malik's witnesses (on a tablet and) (6) enclose (it) in a case, and (8) let (7) the word (8) return to me (6) within (7) 10 days.

(9) I have set (down) (8) the days of . . . (9) for the lads. (10) You yourself (11) had held it up (10) until today(?) . . . (12) On the day (that) (13) you hear (12) [my] message, (15) send(?) (14) whatever (13) lads (15) are available (lit., residing) (14) there. (Line 16 is fragmentary.)

(17) Why (18) do they remain (17) there (18) while you (19) have neither textiles nor (20) wool? Within 10 days (21) prepare yourself (for the journey) and (22) come here and (23) go (22) to Ninashshā. (23) I do not have anyone (there). (26) You have not left (as much as) one shekel's (worth of) merchandise (24) of the 10 manas of tin (25) or the 10 (or 11) textiles (which) I had paid(?) . . .

(27) You should not say the following: (28) I left merchandise!

(29) The silver from my merchandise (30) which you will take (31) should be (30) together (31) in (a package bearing) his seals. (32) The word which (is coming) from (33) the City (of Assur) will arrive. (34) Then (35) write to me at the earliest (34) the message (35) of our father.

Notes on Pa. 20 = L 29–575

Line 1— Inbi-Ištar was also the writer of a number of other texts some of which involve both Ṣilla-Adad and Asshur-malik or, in some cases, one or the other of these two business partners. In all cases where Inbi-Ištar appears, he is the sender of a letter. These pertinent texts are: ATHE 47; BIN 4, 76; BIN 6, 61 and 62; CCT 2, 17a, 18, 19a; CCT 3, 40c; KTH 12 and 13; and TC 1, 43 and 48. Inbi-Ištar's patronymy is given on the case of ATHE 47 where *Sí-in-*[ ] is preserved.

Lines 5f.— For the meaning of this elliptical expression, see CAD A_2 230a, sub. 3c.

Line 8— Collation provides no help at the end of the line.

Line 9— The transliteration of this line follows our collation.

Line 10— Collation adds no information as to what, if anything, is to be restored in the lacuna at the end of the line.

Line 11— There is space on the text for about one sign in the lacuna.

Line 16— Collation unfortunately sheds no light on this line.

Line 20— Collation shows that in all likelihood nothing is lost.

Line 22— J. Lewy (Halil Edhem Memorial Volume, Ankara, 1947, page 14 and HUCA 27 [1956] 20, n. 86) identified Ninašša with classical Nanassos and modern Nenizi about 40 kilometers east of Aksaray and 110 kilometers southwest of Kültepe. The spelling in our text suggests that the final vowel was long.

Line 25— The number is problematic. The scribe may have intended 10 plus word divider or possibly 11.

Collation shows there is space for about one or two signs at the end of the line. The *bu* is not certain. We have rendered the form as a D perfect which is certainly open to question.

Line 26— Probably nothing is to be restored at the end of the line.

Line 33— We take the verb *i-ma-qú-tám* as a G present plus ventive with *awātum* as the subject since no N forms are clearly attested.

Line 35— For *pānītamma*, see GAG Sections 113b and 119h as well as AHw 818b. We may add our OA example of this idiom without *ina* to von Soden's OB example in GAG Section 119h and MA examples in Section 113b.

Pa. 21 = L 29–577

1. *um-ma A-ḫu-wa-qar-ma*
2. *a-na Šu-Bé-lim ù A-mur-*DINGIR
3. *qí-bi-ma a-na Šu-Bé-lim*
4. *qí-bi-*⌜*ma*⌝ 7 MA.NA 18 GÍN
5. KÙ.BABBAR *ṣa-ru-pá-am* / *a-ma-kam*
6. *a-na A-mur-*DINGIR / *šu-qú-ul*
7. *a-ḫi a-ta* / *a-ma-kam* KÙ.BABBAR-*pí*
8. *a-ma-kam* / *dí*!*-šu-um*[ ]
9. *lá i-sà-ḫu-ur-ma*
10. *li-bu-šu lá i-ma-ra-aṣ*

Edge 11. *a-ma-kam* 1 MA.NA KÙ.BABBAR

Rev. 12. *me-eḫ-ra-tim dí-šu-um*

13. *a-na-ku i-Wa-aḫ-šu-ša-na*
14. *i-ba-áb-tí-šu a-lá-qí-ma*
15. *ú-šé-ba-lá-kum* 4 MA.NA
16. KÙ.BABBAR *Šál-ma-A-šur ub-lá-kum*
17. 1 MA.NA 16 GÍN KÙ.BABBAR *ší-im*
18. *be*!*-er-dim tal-qí* / 18 GÍN
19. KÙ.BABBAR *Kà-ni-ší-ú i-dí-nu-ni-kum*
20. *um-ma a-na-ku-ma pì-ri-kà-ni*
21. *ša-am-ma* / *šé-bi*$_4$*-lam*
22. *šu-ma pì-ri-kà-ni lá taš-am*

Edge 23. KÙ.BABBAR *ma-li-ma dí-šu-um*

24. *šu-ma ší-ma-am taš-am*

25. *a-na ṣí-ib-tim*
Left Edge 26. *li-qí-ma dí-šu-um*
27. *a-dí* 5 *u_4-me* KÙ.BABBAR
28. *ú-šé-ba-lá-*[*kum*]

Translation of Pa. 21 = L 29–577

(1) Thus (says) Aḫu-waqar. (3) Speak (2) to Shū-Bēlum and Amur-ilī. (4) Speak (especially) (3) to Shū-Bēlum, (saying): (6) Weigh out (5) there (4) 7 manas (and) 18 shekels of (5) refined silver (6) to Amur-ilī. (7) You (are) my brother. There, (8) give (7) my silver (8) to him there. (9) He should not stay away! Nor (10) should his heart be worried. (11) There (12) give to him the equivalent (of) (11) one mana of silver. (14) I myself will take (it) (13) in Waḫshushana (14) from his merchandise, and (15) I will send (it) to you.

(16) Shalma-Asshur has brought to you (15) 4 manas of (16) silver. (18) You took (17) one mana (and) 16 shekels of silver as the price of (18) the horse(?). (19) The Kanisheans gave to you (18) 18 shekels of (19) silver.

(20) Thus I (said to you): (21) Buy (20) *pirikannū*-textiles, (21) and send (them) to me. (22) If you have not bought the *pirikannū*-textiles, (23) restore the silver and give (it) to him. (24) If you have bought (them), (26) take (them) (25) for profit-making, (26) and give (them) to him.

(28) I will send (27) the silver (28) to you (27) within 5 days.

Notes on Pa. 21 = L 29–577

Line 8— *Dí*!*-šu-um* is to be read *dinšum*, "give to him." The *dí* seems to have been written over something else. There is space for one or two signs in the lacuna.

Line 9— *Lá i-sà-ḫu-ur-ma* is to be derived from the root *saḫārum*, "to stop, stay, go or come around, to make the rounds," since the stem vowel is "u." J. Lewy (OrNS 29 [1960] 22f.) adds "to be delayed, to stay away." Veenhof (AOATT 108 and notes 543 and 547) suggests the additional meanings of "to do something again, to come back to." The lacuna of line 8 interferes with our complete comprehension of this idiom in this text.

Line 10— For the idiom *libbum marāṣum*, "the heart is sick" = "to be worried, anxious," see AHw 609b.

Line 13— On the location of Waḫšušana and its significance as a "country," see J. Lewy HUCA 27 (1956) 45, 64; Halil Edhem Memorial Volume, Ankara, 1947, 13–16. Lewy also noted that most of the copper for the copper trade came from Waḫšušana (H. Edhem Memorial 15).

Lines 17f.— *Šīm be*[!]*-er-dim*. Collation shows the *be* to be squeezed but like the *be* of lines 20 and 22. Two possible translations present themselves for this expression: 1) *birdum* = *wardum* ("slave") and 2) *perdum* ("horse"[?]). For 1), see GKT Sections 13d and 26e and AHw 128a. For 2), see Veenhof AOATT 373 and AHw 855a. Pa. 15:15–18, 31–33 makes it clear that the approximate cost of donkeys was 20 shekels. (See also Garelli AC 192 and 299.) The price of 16 shekels for the *b/perdum* here favors "equine," as von Soden puts it (AHw 855a), considered somewhat inferior to the noble donkey. A slave (*wardum*) usually cost 30 shekels and upward (Garelli AC 316).

Lines 18–22 are treated by Veenhof (AOATT 124) who reads the number in line 18 as 16. Collation shows the number to be 18.

Line 20— For the nature of *pirikannum*, see notes on Pa. 8:28.

Line 24— For the expression *šīmam ša'āmum*, see AOATT 361–366.

Lines 25f.— *Ana ṣibtim laqā'um*. See AOATT 370, n. 502, where Veenhof is unsure of the proper rendering of the associated idiom *kaspam ana ṣibtim laqā'um*. He suggests both "to borrow money on/for payment of interest" and to borrow "as an amount which increases." Our expression implies that the direct object is not *kaspam* but *pirikannī*. Since the agent has used silver to make the purchase of *pirikannī*, our expression must refer to the use to which the textiles will be put, namely, to be sold for the purpose of making a profit which fits Veenhof's second suggestion.

Pa. 22 = L 29–579

1. *um-ma Im-dí-lúm-ma*
2. *a-na A-šur-*DU$_{10}$ *qí-*⸢*bi*$_4$*-*⸣*ma*
3. 2 GÚ 2 MA.NA AN.[NA]
4. *ú* 5 [$^{túg?}$*ku-*]*ta-ni* SIG$_5$
5. *ku-nu-ki-a* / *A-du na-áš-a-*[*kum*[!]]

6. 15 1/2 GÍN AN.NA 1 LÁ 1/4 GÍN
7. KÙ.BABBAR *a-qá-tí-šu a-dí-šum*
8. *a-ta a-ma-kam mì-ma*
9. *lá ta-da-šu-≪šu-≫ma*
10. *a-na* AN.NA-*ki-a* 6 GÍN TA
11. *a-na* TÚG-*ba-tí-a* 15 GÍN TA *iš-tí* AN.NA
12. *a-na i-ta-aṭ-lim dí-in*
13. *šu-ma lá ki-a-am* AN.NA-*ki*
Edge 14. *i-ku-nu-ki-šu-ma*
15. *li-bi$_4$-ší ú* [*a-*]*dí*
Rev. 16. *ma-lá ú ší-ni-šu*
17. *ú-za-kà áp-tí ki-ma*
18. AN.NA-*ku i-ša-du-du-ni*
19. *ú-za-kà áp-tí a-ta*
20. *i-na ṭup-pì-kà*
21. *ta-ša-pá-*<*ra-*>*am um-ma*
22. *a-ta-ma* 7 GÍN TA AN.NA-*kà*
23. *a-tí-dí-in šu-ma* AN.NA
24. *i-ba-ší-ma lá ta-tí-dí-in*
25. *tí-ir-ta-kà li-li-*⸢*kam*⸣
26. *li-bi$_4$ lá i-ma-ra-aṣ*
27. *ú šu-ma ta-tí-dí-in*
28. KÙ.BABBAR *ṣa-ru-pá-am*
29. KÙ.BABBAR-*áp qí-ip-tim*
Edge 30. *ku-nu-uk-ma*
Left Edge 31. *šé-bi$_4$-lam ú ṣú-ba-tí-a*
32. 15 GÍN TA

Translation of Pa. 22 = L 29–579

(1) Thus (says) Imdīlum: (2) Speak to Asshur-ṭāb, (saying), (5) Adū is carrying [to you] (3) two talents (and) two manas of tin(!) (4) as well as 5 cloths of good quality (5) (bearing) my seals. (7) I have given into his hand (6) 15 1/2 shekels of tin (and) 3/4 of a shekel of (7) silver. (8) As for you there, (9) do not give (8) anything (9) to him. But (12) convert into cash (10) my tin at a rate of 6 shekels (per one shekel of silver and) (11) my cloths at the rate of (one) per 15 shekels (of silver) along with the tin. (13) If (you) cannot (do) so, (15) let (13) my tin (15) remain (14) in packages bearing his seals. (15f.) Repeatedly (17) I will

(be able to) clear (it at a profit). I have opened (it). When (18) they pull the tin out, (19) I will clear (it).

(19) I opened (your letter). You (21) wrote (20) in your letter (21f.) saying: (23) I sold (22) your tin at 7 shekels per (one shekel of silver). (23) If (24) there is (23) tin (available) (24) and you have not sold (it), (25) let your instruction come to me. (26) Let my heart not become anxious. (27) But if you have sold (it), (30) seal (28) the refined silver, (29) (that is,) the investment silver (30) and (31) send (it) to me as well as (the silver derived from selling) my cloths (32) at the rate of 15 shekels per (cloth).

Notes on Pa. 22 = L 29–579

Line 5— The PN Adu is reasonably well known spelled either as *A-du* or *A-du-ú*.

Line 6— Mrs. Lewy drew 1 1/4 as the second number. Collation favors 1 LÁ 1/4 = 3/4 The GÍN is partially visible on the tablet.

Line 7— Collation shows the *šum* is on the text.

Line 12— For the idiom *ana itaṭlim nadānum*, see the note on Pa. 14:6 above.

Line 14— The *ki* in *kunukkišuma* is written like the one in line 13.

Line 15— *Li-bi*$_4$*-ší* must be taken as a precative from *bašā'um*. See GKT Section 84d.

Line 16— The idiom *mala u šinīšu* is translated "once or twice" by von Soden (AHw 592b) and "repeatedly" by Hecker (GKT Section 71a). The expression with *adi* prefixed appears in TC 3, 73:2. The *a* of *adi* is not perfect but likely after collation.

Line 18— Collation shows that the *ku* of AN.NA-*ku* is clear, which creates somewhat of a problem by suggesting that "tin" was written as the subject of the verb *išaddudūni*. But *šadādum* ("to pull, draw") has no passive or stative meaning for the G stem.

Šadādum is infrequent in OA with only 5 other occurrences known to me. See GKT Sections 40f and 78d as well as AHw 1121b.

Line 29— For the meaning of *qīptum*, see the note on Pa. 6:33 above. Mrs. Lewy's published line drawing shows two additional lines of text following line 32 which repeat lines 31f. Collation shows that these repeated lines are not a part of the text and were repeated in HUCA by a modern scribal error.

Pa. 23 A = L 29–580 Inner Tablet

1. 2 1/3 MA.NA 5 GÍN KÙ.BABBAR
2. *ṣa-ru-pá-am i-ṣé-er*
3. *A-ba-tim ù Ku-ki-ni-im*
4. *me-er-i-šu A-ḫu-qar*
5. *i-šu iš-tù ḫa-muš-tim*
6. *ša qá-tí* dMAR.TU-*ba-ni*
7. *ù A-šur-na-da*
8. *a-na 8 ḫa-am-ša-tim*

Edge 9. *i-ša-qal*

10. *šu-ma lá iš-qú-ul*

Rev. 11. *i*-ITI KAM / *a-na*

12. 1 MA.NA-*im*
13. 1 1/2 GÍN TA *ṣí-ib-tám*
14. *ú-ṣa-áb* ITI KAM
15. *ṣí-ip-im li-mu-um*
16. *A-šur-na-da*
17. DUMU *Púzur-A-na*
18. IGI *A-šur-iš-ta-kál*
19. IGI dIM-ILLAT

Edge 20. IGI *En-um-A-šur*

Pa. 23 B = L 29–630 + L 29–585 = L 29–580 Case

1′. [*Ku-ki-n*]*i-im me-er-i-šu*
2′. [2 1/3 MA.]NA 5 GÍN KÙ.BABBAR
3′. [*ṣa-ru-pá-a*]*m i-ṣé-er*
4′. [*A-ba-tí*]*m ú Ku-ki-nim*
5′. [*me-er-*]*i-šu* / *A-ḫu-qar*!
6′. [*i-šu*] *iš-tù ḫa-muš-*[*tim*]
7′. *ša qá-tí* dMAR.TU-*ba-ni*
8′. *ù A-šur-na-da a-na* 8!
9′. *ḫa-am-ša-tim i-ša-qal*
10′. *šu-ma lá iš-qú-ul a-na*
11′. 1 MA.NA-*im i-na* ITI KAM
12′. 1 1/2 GÍN TA *ṣí-ib-tám*
13′. *ù-ṣa-áb* ITI KAM *ṣí-ip-im*
14′. *li-mu-um*

[The rest broken]

Note: Lines 1′–6′ appear on L 29–630; lines 7′–14′, on L 29–585.

Translation of Pa. 23 A = L 29–580 Tablet

(4) Aḫu-(wa)qar (5) has (a debt of) (1) 2 1/3 manas (and) 5 shekels of (2) refined (1) silver (2) against (3) Abatum or Kukinum, (4) his son. (5) From the *ḫamushtum*-period (6) of the successor of Amurrum-bāni (7) and Asshur-nādā (9) he shall weigh (it) out (8) within 8 *ḫamushtum*-periods. (10) If he has not weighed (it) out (on time), (14) he shall add (13) 1 1/2 shekels (11) per month, per (12) mana (as) (13) interest. (14) (Dated from) the month of (15) Ṣip'um, the eponymy (of) (16) Asshur-nādā (17) son of Puzur-Ana. (18) In the presence of Asshurish-takal, (19) in the presence of Adad-ellāt, (20) in the presence of Enna-Asshur.

Translation of Pa. 23 B = L 29–630 + L 29–585 = L 29-580 Case

(The list of seal impressions of the witnesses and of the debtors is missing.)

(5′) Aḫu-(wa)qar (6′) [has (a debt of) (2′) 2 1/3 ma]nas (and) 5 shekels of [(3′) refined] (2′) silver (3′) against [(4′) Abat]um or Kukinum, (5′) his [son]. (6′) From the *ḫamush[tum*-period] (7′) of the successor of Amurrum-bāni (8′) and Asshur-nādā (9′) he shall weigh (it) out (8′) within 8(!) (9′) *ḫamushtum*-periods. (10′) If he has not weighed (it) out (on time), (13′) he shall add (12′) interest at the rate of 1 1/2 shekels (10′) per (11′) mana per month. (13′) (Dated from) the month of Ṣip'um, (14′) the eponymy (of) [Asshur-nādā son of Puzur-Ana.]

Notes on Pa. 23 A = L 29–580 Tablet

Line 3— Since the verbs in lines 9, 10, and 14 are singular as are the same verbs on the Case, *ù* may be considered to be *ū*, "or" (see GKT Section 104b).

The PN Abatum is attested in EL 155:20 (= VAT 13480). ICK 1, 177:11 has *A-ba-ta-na-nim* which may be a related PN.

Kukinum is unknown to me elsewhere.

Lines 6f. and 15ff.— The *ḫamuštum*-period of Amurrum-bāni and Asshur-nādā is previously attested, as is the eponymy of Asshur-nādā.

Notes on Pa. 23 B = L 29–630 + L 29–585 = L 29–580 Case

Line 8′— The number on the text is fragmentary; 7 of the 8 wedges are preserved.

Line 12′— Collation shows the GÍN is followed by TA.

Pa. 24 = L 29–581

1. *a-na A-šùr-na-da*
2. *ù* ^{d}UTU-*tap-pá-i qí-bi$_4$-ma*
3. *um-ma I-ṣí-me-a-ma*
4. *a-na A-šùr-na-da qí-bi$_4$-ma*
5. *sú-ub-ri / wa-áš-ba-at-ma*
6. *iš-tí / a-ni-ú-tim*
7. *a-na wa-ṣa-e-ma*
8. *ḫu-zi-ru-um / e-gi$_5$-ri-ma*

Edge 9. *am-qú-ut-ma / šé-pì*

10. *áš-tí-bi$_4$-ir-ma*

Rev. 11. *ak-ta-lá / bé-ú-lá-tim*

12. *ša / Púzur-A-šùr*
13. DUMU *En-nam-A-šùr*
14. *a-na-ku ù* ^{d}UTU-*tap-pá-i*
15. *ú-lá nu-kà-al / a-na a-i-tim*
16. *wa-ar-dí ú-kà-lu*
17. *be-li a-ta* ^{d}UTU *a-ta*
18. ^{d}UTU-*tap-pá-i*
19. *ṣa-ba-at-ma / šé-ri-a-šu*

Edge 20. *a-na na-ṣa-ar*

21. *sú-ub-ri-a / ma-ma-an*
22. *lá-šu-ú*

Left Edge 23. *a-bi$_4$ a-ta / i-lá na-ṣí-ri-im*

24. *sú-ub-ri*
25. *lá i-ḫa-li-iq*

Translation of Pa. 24 = L 29–581

(2) Speak (1) to Asshur-nādā (2) and Shamash-tappā'ī, (3) thus (says) Iṣime'a. (4) Speak to Asshur-nādā (saying): (5) My servant is staying at home and (8) a boar charged me (7) when I was leaving

(6) with these (people, or articles) (8) and (9) I fell and (10) broke (9) my foot (10) and (11) I have been confined.

(14) I and Shamash-tappā'ī (15) are not holding back (11) the interest-free investment capital (12) of Puzur-Asshur (13) son of Enna-Asshur; (so) (15) why (16) are they holding my slave? (17) You (are) my lord; you (are) my sun! (19) Seize (18) Shamash-tappā'ī (19) and send him here! (22) There is (21) no one (20) to watch over (21) my servant. (23) You (are) my father! (24) My servant (25) must not be lost (23) through lack of surveillance!

Notes on Pa. 24 = L 29–581

Line 2— Note the *ma* which was written at the end of the following line.

Lines 5, 21, and 24— On *subrum* = "domestic servant," see H. and J. Lewy HUCA 38 (1967) 1–15 and AHw 1108a.

Line 6— *Išti anni'ūtim*, "from these," is strange. Perhaps the demonstrative pronoun's antecedent is an indefinite "people" or "articles for trade."

Line 8— Collation shows the *ḫu* at the beginning of the line is all right.

Ḫuzirum e-KI-*ri-ma* is difficult. Kramer in reporting on this text in his brief foreword (HUCA 39 [1968] 2) used "charge," which seems to have come from a three-page typed general commentary of Mrs. Lewy's on some interesting features of these texts. The origin of Kramer's donkey is unknown to me.

The verbal root seems to be *egārum*, "to twist, be twisted." CAD E 42 (sub 1. c)) suggests the derived meanings of "to be perverse, cross" and "to maneuver for position" (sub 1.e)). AHw 190 shows that the G stem may describe the aggressive action of animals. In our context, "to charge" may be a little too specific; "to attack" suggests hostility without attempting to designate the exact action of the boar. It does not appear in this context that the boar wounded Iṣime'a, but that it caused him to fall and break his foot or leg.

Line 17— ^{d}UTU *atta* is unusual. See AHw 1159a for two OA examples of this expression.

Lines 18–25 are treated by H. and J. Lewy HUCA 38 (1967) 9, and n. 46.

Line 23— Note the vowel harmony, *naṣārim* > *naṣīrim*, in the G infinitive.

Pa. 25 = L 29–583

	1.	*um-ma Ili*$_5$*-mì-tí-ma*
	2.	*a-na A-šùr-*GAL *ù*
	3.	*A-šur-i-mì-tí qí-bi-ma*
	4.	*a-na A-šùr-*GAL *qí-bi*$_4$*-ma*
	5.	*lá li-bi*$_4$ / ⌜DINGIR-⌝*ma*
	6.	DU$_{10}$-*A-šùr* DUMU *a-ḫi-kà*
	7.	*me-et ki-ma me-tù*
	8.	*a-lik*$^{ik!}$ / *e-er-šu-šu*
	9.	*aṣ-ba-at-ma*
Edge	10.	*ú ḫu-ur-*<*ší-*>*a-an-šu*
Rev.	11.	*i-li-bi*$_4$ *Lá-qí-pì-im*
	12.	*a-ḫi-šu* ≪*aṣ*≫
	13.	*aṣ-ba-at ù* KÙ.BABBAR
	14.	1 MA.NA *i-li-bi*$_4$
	15.	DAM.GAR-*ru-tim ba-áb-ta-šu*
	16.	*aṣ-ba-at i-na* <*ša-*>*am-ší*
	17.	*ṭup-pì ta*$^!$*-ša-me-ú*
	18.	*lá ta-bi*$_4$*-ad* / *a-tal-kam*
	19.	*šu-ma a-ma-kam lá-šu*
Edge	20.	*a-šar*$^!$ *wa-áš-bu*
	21.	*šu-[pu-]ur-[šu-]um*
Left Edge	22.	DUMU *I-dí-Ku-bi*$_4$*-im*
	23.	*lá té-zi-ba-am*
	24.	*iš-tí Kur-ub-Ištar ṭur*$_4$*-da-šu*

Translation of Pa. 25 = L 29–583

(1) Thus (says) Ilī-(i)mittī, (3) speak (2) to Asshur-rabi and (3) Asshur-imittī; (4) speak (especially) to Asshur-rabi, (saying): (5) Unfortunately(?) (6) Ṭāb-Asshur, your brother's son, (7) is dead. Since (he) is dead, (8) come (here)! (9) I have seized (8) his bed(?) (9) and (13) I have (10) also (13) seized (10) his bundle (11) from Lā-qēpum, (12) his brother. (13) Furthermore, (16) I have seized (14) one mana (of) (13) silver, (15) his assets, (14) from (15) the merchandise.

(16) On the (very) day (17) you hear my tablet, (18) do not delay even one night; come here!

(19) If he (Asshur-rabi) is not there, (21) you (Asshur-imittī) write

to him (20) wherever he is residing. (23) Do not leave (22) Īdī-Kubum's son (23) behind; (24) send him with Kurub-Ishtar.

Notes on Pa. 25 = L 29–583

Lines 2–4— The message is meant for Asshur-rabi; Asshur-imittī is co-addressee in case Asshur-rabi is absent when the letter arrives. See lines 19–21.

Line 5— The end of line 5 is somewhat damaged. We restore *lā libbi ilimma* on the basis of examples cited in CAD L 172a with the meaning "the god was unwilling; so PN died" = "unfortunately PN died." The DINGIR is not certain, however.

Line 8— This whole line is problematic. It appears that the scribe wrote something, changed his mind, and wrote something else over it. The beginning appears to be  = *a-lik*[ik!] plus word divider. J. Lewy's 1956 collation suggests that the scribe wrote  first and then changed it to *li*, 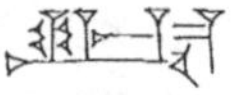 , which was followed by *ik-ma*[?]. The *ma*[?] looks more like *e*, however. The best I can do with it is as it is rendered in the transliteration above.

Additional suspicion is created by the following *e-er-šu-šu*, "his bed," since the verb *aṣbat* in line 9 requires its object in the accusative. With no better suggestion, we must assume scribal error as in lines 10, 12, 16, and 17. These errors suggest haste due to the urgency and emotional upheaval of the circumstances surrounding the writing of this letter.

Line 11— Collation shows the *qí* is certain.

Line 12— The scribe did not completely erase the *aṣ* on line 12.

Line 15— On the abstract form *tamkaruttum*, see GKT Section 57d. This abstract also appears in EL 290:y + 2 (= KTP 19); 316:10 (= Giessen 1–5 = KUG 12); and ICK 1, 17b:29. The term may designate the organization of the merchants.

Line 17— According to H. Lewy's 1967 collation, the troublesome sign beginning the verb looks like UR, although J. Lewy in 1956 had read *ta*. The reading UR = *taš* in OA is attested in Gelb 34:12; 35:4; and Pa. 21:22, 24. If the scribe intended to write *taššamme'u*, however, another problem is created because the N stem is completely out of place in this context. Collation shows the sign to be *ta*, though it is strangely written, 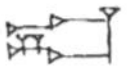 . The *ta* in line 15 is no help here since it is severely squeezed on the end of the line around the edge.

Line 21— We follow here the reconstruction of J. Lewy in WO 2 (1959) 434, n. 6. Collation was of no help in making the reconstruction more sure.

Pa. 26 = L 29–584

1. *Púzur-Ištar / a-na*
2. ^{d}IM-SIPA *iṣ-ba-at-ni-a-tí-ma*
3. *um-ma Púzur-Ištar-ma*
4. *a-na* ^{d}IM-SIPA-*ma*
5. 7 2/3 MA.NA $3^{!}$ GÍN KÙ.BABBAR
6. *i-na l[i-bi-kà] i-ba-ší*
7. *lá i-ba-ší / ú-ul ik-ri*
8. *ú-ul kà-i-ni um-ma*
9. ^{d}IM-SIPA-*ma / a-na*
10. *Puzúr-Ištar-ma / ki-na*
11. 7 2/3 MA.NA 3 GÍN KÙ.BABBAR
Edge 12. *ší-im pá-ra-kà-ni-kà*
13. *ša a-sú-ḫu*
Rev. 14. *ù* 1 MA.NA KÙ.BABBAR *ša*
15. *a-na be-a-lim / ta-dí-na-*<*ni*>
16. *i-na li-bi*$_4$*-a i-ba-ší*
17. *um-ma Puzúr-Ištar-ma* KÙ.BABBAR-*pì*
18. *dí-nam um-ma* ^{d}IM-SIPA-*ma*
19. *a-na Puzúr-Ištar-ma ḫu-ur-ší-a-ni*
20. *šé-ṣí-a-ma lu* URUDU */ lu ší-im*
21. ANŠE *ša tal-qí-ú* <*dí-nam*>
22. *ḫu-ur-ší-a-šu / Puzúr-Ištar*
23. *ú-šé-ṣí-a-ma* 4 MA.NA U[RUDU]
24. KÙ.BABBAR/ *ša ḫur*$^{!}$*-ší-a-ni-šu*
Edge 25. *a-na Puzúr-Ištar is-ni-iq*
26. *lu* KÙ.BABBAR *lu ší-im* 2 GÚ
27. URUDU *lá-mu-nim*
Left Edge 28. *lu ší-im* 1/$2^{?}$ GÚ URUDU DU$_{10}$
29. *lu ší-im* ANŠE 15 GÍN KÙ.BABBAR
30. *i-dí-nu*

Translation of Pa. 26 = L 29–584

(1) Puzur-Ishtar (2) called our court into session (literally, seized us) (1) against (2) Adad-rē'um and (3) thus Puzur-Ishtar (said) (4) to Adad-rē'um: (6) Are (5) 7 2/3 manas (and) 3(!) shekels of silver (6) in your account (7) or not? Either deny (it to) me (8) or confirm it (for) me!

(8) Thus (says) (9) Adad-rē'um to (10) Puzur-Ishtar: It is true! (16) In my account are (11) 7 2/3 manas (and) 3 shekels of silver, (12) the price of your *pirikannū*-textiles, (13) which I removed, (14) and also one mana of silver, which (15) you gave (me) for interest-free investment.

(17) Thus (says) Puzur-Ishtar: (18) Give me (17) my silver!

(18) Thus Adad-rē'um (said) (19) to Puzur-Ishtar: (20) Bring out (19) my bundle (20) and (21) give me(!) (20) either copper or the price of (21) the donkey which you took.

(22) Puzur-Ishtar (23) brought forth (22) his bundle (23) and (25) he checked (off) for Puzur-Ishtar (23) 4 manas of copper's (worth of) (24) silver. (30) They sold (26) either silver or the price of 2 talents of (27) poor quality copper (28) or the price of 1/2(?) talent of good-quality copper (29) or the price of a donkey, (namely) 15 shekels of silver.

Notes on Pa. 26 = L 29–584

Line 2— The last two signs were written at the end of line 3.

Lines 1, 3, 10, 17, 19, 22, and 25— Note that the scribe felt free to interchange the two spellings of *Puzur* in writing the same person's name.

Lines 6f.— For the expression *ibašši lā ibašši*, "either there is or there is not . . .", see GKT Section 129a.

Lines 7f.— For *ul . . . ul*, "either . . . or," see GKT Section 116a.

Lines 12f.— The *kà* which appears to belong at the end of line 13 should be read at the end of line 12 although minimal space is placed between it and the *ḫu*.

Line 15— We would expect the verb to be a subjunctive since it follows *ša*. Two possibilities present themselves: either *ta-dí-nu*! or *ta-dí-na-*<*ni*>. Collation confirms the word divider.

Line 21— Although the text clearly has nothing inscribed following *ša talqi'u*, a verb with the general meaning of *dinam* must be assumed, otherwise the second person of *talqi'u* cannot be fitted into the sentence.

Line 22— Collation shows the word divider is possible but not certain.

Line 29— Note the KÙ.BABBAR written at the end of line 30.

Pa. 27 = L 29–586

1. *a-na Ḫa-šu-ša-ar-na*
2. *qí-bi-ma um-ma*
3. *A-šur-ták-lá-ku ù*
4. *I-dí-*^{d}UTU *i-ša-am-ší*
5. *na-áš-pe-er-tí-ni*
6. *ta-ša-me-i-ni*
7. *tí-ib-e-ma / a-na*
8. *Té-ga-ra-ma a-ta-al-ki-im*
9. *i-na Té-ga-ra-ma*

Edge 10. *i-ša-ḫa-at*

Rev. 11. *tí-ir-tí-a lu-uš*$^{!}$*-ba*$^{!}$*-tí*

12. *a-dí e-tí-qá-ni*
13. *i-ša-am-ší ta-ta-li-ki-ni*
14. *tí-ir-tí-ki*
15. *li-li-kam*
16. *a-ta-al-ki-im-ma*
17. [KÙ.BABBAR] / *i-na Wa-aḫ-šu-ša-na*
18. *kà-i-li* / [ ] ZU$^{?}$

Edge 19. *I-dí-*^{d}UTU DUMU$^{?}$

20. *a-na*$^{?}$ *ma*$^{?}$ [ ] *ta*$^{?}$ x

Left Edge 21. [ ] *lá*$^{?}$ [ ]

22. *I-dí-*^{d}UTU *ri*$^{?}$ [ ]
23. [ ] *tim*$^{?}$

Translation of Pa. 27 = L 29–586

(2) Speak (1) to Ḫashusharna. (2) Thus (says) (3) Asshur-taklāku and (4) Īdī-Shamash. On the very day (6) you hear (5) our message (7) arise and (8) come (7) to (8) Tegarama. (11) Remain (9) in Tegarama (10) responsible for (11) my instruction. (12) Until I come, (13) on the

(very) day you come (15) let your (14) instruction (15) come to me. (16) (Then) come here and (18) hold (17) the silver(?) from Waḫshushana. (The rest of the text is broken except for the PN, Īdī-Shamash, in lines 19 and 22.)

Notes on Pa. 27 = L 29–586

Line 1— The feminine PN, Ḫašušarna, is attested in EL 5:8, 12, and 19 (= TCL 1, 242) where a certain Ḫašušarna daughter of Udgaria was divorced by her husband, Talia. Otherwise the PN is unknown to me. See Garelli AC 143.

Line 4— Note the missing *ma* of the *umma* PN *ma* address formula following the PN.

Line 8— Tegarama as a GN occurs in OA only rarely: KUG 24:3; KTS 51b:6!; BIN 6, 136:11f.; CCT 5, 3b:9!, 10. Garelli (AC 117f.) discussed its location based on CCT 1, 29:10 and CCT 3, 44b:8. J. Lewy (HUCA 33 [1962] 52–55; HUCA 27 [1956] 22, n. 95; HUCA 23/1 [1950/51] 367, n. 33) argued that Tegarama was in the vicinity of Ḫurrama, Taišama, Mama, Ullama, Kuššara, Baraddum, and Ḫarana and that this cluster of cities and towns was to be sought in East Anatolia southeast of Kaniš in the area of Elbistan. He further maintained that the biblical equivalent of Tegarama was תוגרמה. In JAOS 57 (1937) 435 J. Lewy restored Tegarama in line 30 of Gelb 58. The mention of Waḫšušana in our text along with Tegarama is most intriguing since Lewy maintained that Waḫšušana's locale was to be found southwest of Kaniš (H. Edhem Memorial 13–16). Unfortunately Pa. 27 becomes fragmentary at this point so that we cannot determine the relationship of the two places. The situation is further complicated by our ignorance of Ḫašušarna's residence when she received this letter. Neither can we determine the point of origin of the letter. Because of the apparently large distance between Tegarama and Waḫšušana we translate *ina* in line 17 as "from" instead of "in."

Line 10— *I-ša-ḫa-at*, "at the side of," "responsible for." See AHw 1129 as well as the note on Pa. 14:19 above.

Line 11— Our rendering of the latter part of this line is favored, but not made certain, by collation. The *uš* is likely, although *ta* is less sure with the upper *Winkelhaken* damaged. The next sign, probably *ba*, is not intact either.

We take *uš-ba-tí* as a G stative of *wašābum*. For *lū* plus stative as an alternate means of expressing a command, see GKT Section 77a.

Hecker (GKT Section 93e) cites ATHE 41:7 (*ušbāku*) as an example of *uš* alternating with *waš* in the stative of this verb.

Line 17— Collation shows the last part of BABBAR remains.

Lines 18–23— Collation offers no help on these fragmentary lines. The DUMU of line 19 may be *i*.

Pa. 28 = L 29–587

1. *a-na Púzur-A-šur qí-bi₄-ma*
2. *um-ma Ili₅-we-da-ku-ma*
3. *ki-ma* ZI.GA-*tù-ni-ma*
4. *ù ḫa-ra-nu-um da-na-at-ni*
5. *Ḫu-ud-kà lá aṭ-ru-da-am*
6. *ki-ma ḫa-ra-nu-um i-ší-ru-ma*
7. *a-li-ku pá-ni-ú-tum iš-li-mu-ni-ni*
8. KÙ.BABBAR 1 MA.NA *lu ku-a-am*
9. *lu i-a-am uš-ta-ṣa-b*[*a-a*]*t-ma*
10. *Ḫu-ud-kà a-ṭa-ra-dam*
11. *a-ma-lá* ⌜*ta-*⌝*áš-pu-ra-ni*
12. KÙ.BABBAR *a-na a-lim*^ki *šé-bi₄-il₅-ma*
13. *ší-ma-am li-iš-ú-mu-nim*

Edge

14. *a-dí Ku-zi-im*
15. *ša ta-áš-pu-ra-ni*

Rev.

16. *i-na Du-ur-ḫu-mì-id*
17. *Ku-zu-um wa-ša-áb*
18. *ù tí-ir-tí a-ṣé-ri-šu*
19. *i-ta-lá-ak um-ma a-na-ku-ma*
20. TÚG^ḫi.a *ša Púzur-A-šùr*
21. 20 TÚG SIG₅ 31 TÚG *ša qá-tim*
22. 3 ANŠE *ṣa-lá-mì a-na ša ki-ma*
23. *Puzúr-A-šùr pì-qí-id*
24. *a-na-ku mì-ma lá ṭá-ḫu-a-ku*
25. *a-ma-kam šu-pu-ur-ma*
26. *a-na ša ki-ma ku-wa*^!*-tí* 20 TÚG SIG₅
27. ≪SIG₅≫ 31 TÚG *ša qá-tim*
28. *ù* 3 ANŠE *ṣa-lá-mì*
29. *a-na* <*ša*> *ki-ma ku-wa-tí*

Edge

30. *li-ip-qí-id-ma*
31. *ú šu-wa-tí a-ṣé-ri-a*

Left Edge

32. *ṭù-ur-da-šu a-bi₄ a-ta ší-tí*

33. TÚG^{ḫi} *ša Da-na-A-šùr*
34. *ša-dí-šu-ma a-qá-tí-a*
35. *li-bi$_4$-ší-ú*

Translation of Pa. 28 = L 29–587

(1) Speak to Puzur-Asshur. (2) Thus (says) Ilī-wedāku: (3) Since you are indisposed and (4) further the road is difficult, (5) I have not sent Ḫudka. (6) As soon as the road has become normal and (7) the first messengers have (arrived) safely, (9) I will seize (8) one mana (of) silver, either yours (9) or mine, and (10) I will send Ḫudka (with it).

(11) According to what you wrote, (12) send the silver to the City (of Assur) and (13) let them make purchases.

(14) As to Kuzum (15) about (whom) you wrote, (17) Kuzum is residing (16) in Durḫumid; (18) so my instruction (19) went (18) to him (19) saying: (23) Entrust (20) the textiles of Puzur-Asshur, (namely), (21) 20 good-quality textiles, 31 average-quality textiles (and) (22) 3 black donkeys to (23) Puzur-Asshur's (22) representative. (24) As for me, I am not involved whatsoever. (25) There write and (30) let him entrust (26) to your representative 20 good-quality textiles, (27) 31 average-quality textiles (28) and 3 black donkeys (29) to your representative (30) and (32) send him (31) to me. (32) You (are) my father! (34) Make him sell (32) the rest of (33) the textiles belonging to Danna-Asshur (34) and (35) let them be (34) in my account!

Notes on Pa. 28 = L 29–587

Line 3— ZI.GA-*tù-ni-ma* is difficult as indicated by Veenhof (AOATT 330, n. 445) who offers other examples of the idiom without hazarding a guess as to its meaning beyond expressing doubt as to "army" in CAD A_2 358b. We may add several possibilities: 1) *sikkatum*, "sickness" (AHw 1042a), 2) some substantive from *sakākum*, "to stop up" (AHw 1010b), in the sense of stating that the roads and passes are blocked because of the winter weather, 3) a G stative subjunctive from *si'āqum*, "to be narrow, small, to be in distress." We have followed the latter suggestion in spite of the fact that it does not account for all of Veenhof's examples. Our reasoning is that the other two possibilities fit our context less well. Nor must we assume that all Veenhof's examples come from the same root.

Line 4— Collation shows *ù* is correct.

We follow Veenhof (AOATT 330) for the expression *ḫarrānum dannatni*, "the road/journey is difficult."

Lines 6–9 are rendered by Veenhof AOATT 330 and 331, n. 446 (for the root *ešārum*, "to become normal"). CAD Ṣ 39 translates the Št stem of *ṣabātum* as "to assemble, collect," which we favor over Veenhof's rendering.

Collation verifies our reading *ki-ma*.

Lines 14 and 17— The PN Kuzum is known in CCT 1, 16a:4; CCT 2, 16a:9; BIN 6, 10:1 (*Ku-zu-ú*), 16 (*Ku-zu*), Case 2 (ib.), 3 (ib.); 114:14 (*Ku-zu-um*); 130:9 (ib.); 146:3 (ib.); and ATHE 44:34.

Collation shows that the *ku* of line 14 is correct and that the reading *Ku-zu-um* of line 17 is clear.

Line 16— See H. Lewy JCS 17 (1963) 103f. for a summary of the evidence for the location of Durḫumid.

Line 21— For *ša qātim* = "average-quality," see the note on Pa. 15:8.

Line 24— For the meaning of *ṭaḫā'um*, see OACP 20 and 73 as well as EL II p. 192, n. 2.

Line 26— The *wa* of *ku-wa-tí* is slightly broken.

Line 33— Collation verifies the reading of the PN as *Da-na-A-šùr*.

Pa. 29 = L 29–588

1. *a-na A-ḫa-tim*
2. *qí-bi*$_4$*-ma um-ma Púzur-*DINGIR*-ma*
3. *a-dí* KÙ.BABBAR *ša Ma-nu-um-*<*ba-lúm* or *ki-*>*A-šur*
4. *um-mì a-tí be-el-tí a-tí*
5. *a-na Ša-lá-tù-wa-ar*
6. *ú-lá ú-šu-ru*
7. *a-wa-tum da-na*
8. KÙ.BABBAR *šu-qú-li-ma*
9. *a-wi-lam*$_5$ *lam-na-am*

Edge 10. *i-ṣé-ri-a ṭa!-ḫi!*

Rev. 11. *a-dí* ITI KAM *iš-tí-in*

12. *a-wa-tum i-za-ku-a-ni*
13. *i-nu-mì ša a-lá-kà-ni*
14. KÙ.BABBAR *ù ṣí-ba-sú*
15. *ša Ḫa-ṣa-áb-ṣi-li-im*

16. *lá ta-ga-mì-li-ni*
17. *i-ṣé-ri-a li-qí*
18. *ší-im pì-ri-kà-ni*
19. *a-na-kam ba-at-qú*
20. *ma-ḫi-ir Kà-ni-ìš lá ma-ṣí*
Edge 21. *a-na ≪a≫ u_4-um*
22. *e-ṭá-ri-im*
Left Edge 23. *a-šu-mì* LÚ? *ta-áp-qí-da*
24. *lá ta-áp-qí!-da*
25. *úz-ni pì-tí tí-ir-tí-ki*
26. *a-ni-tum lá a-ni-tum*
27. *lí-lí-kam*

Translation of Pa. 29 = L 29–588

(2) Speak (1) to Aḫatum. (2) Thus (says) Puzur-ilum: (3) In regard to Mannum-<balum or, kī->Asshur's silver, (4) you (are) my mother; you (are) my "boss" (mistress)! (6) They will not release (it) (5) at (or, to) Shalatuwar. (7) The matter (is) grave! (8) Weigh out the silver and (10) make (9) (that) evil man (10) approach me! (11) In one month's time (12) the affairs will clear up. (13) When I come, (16) will you not do me a favor regarding (14) the silver and its interest (15) belonging to Ḫaṣab-ṣillum? (17) Take (it) over for me! (18) The price of the *pirikannū*-textiles (19) (is) low here, (20) (and) the market-price at Kanish is not high enough. (23) Either you entrusted (them) for the gentleman (21) while (22) he could still be saved financially (or) (24) you did not entrust (them). (25) Open my ear! (27) Let (25) your instruction (27) come to me (26) whether (you did) or not!

Notes on Pa. 29 = L 29–588

Line 1— Aḫatum as a business lady is known from a limited number of texts. Only one Aḫatum is known by patronym, the *gubabtum*-priestess daughter of Ilī-bāni son of Ija, from ICK 1, 12. In TC 2, 67:9 (= EL 205) we have an Aḫatum who is wife of Aḫuni son of Šu-Ištar. See also MAH 16312 (Garelli RA 59 [1965] 34f.); BIN 4, 153:3 (= EL 75); 183:4 (= EL 214); CCT 4, 15a:1; KTS 49c:17 (= EL 135; *Za-ḫa-tim*, perhaps to be read *A!-ḫa-tim*); and 45b:4 (= EL 58).

Line 3— The PN *Ma-nu-um-A-šur* is a mistake for Mannum-balum-Asshur or Mannum-kī-Asshur since Mannum-Asshur is unattested.

Line 5— According to J. Lewy (H. Edhem Memorial [1947] 14) Šalatuwar was situated on the Waḫšušana-Burušḫaddum road west of Kaniš and was the seat of a *wubartum* (HUCA 27 [1956] 20, n. 85; 59, n. 251; 64).

Line 7— Collation shows that nothing is missing at the end of the line, nor is there an erasure. For *awātum danna*, see CAD D 98a.

Line 10— Collation has not clarified the crux at the end of the line. The sign we have read TA = *ṭá* looks like *uš*. Neither is the *ḫì* perfect. We have read *ṭá*!-*ḫi*! chiefly because it makes a readable text while *uš-ḫi* and *uš-kam* do not.

Line 13— *Inūmī ša* . . . is odd; *inūmī* usually occurs without the relative conjunction.

Line 15— The PN Ḫaṣab-ṣillum is unknown to me elsewhere in OA.

Line 17— For the idiom *iṣṣer laqā'um* = "to take over for," see AOATT 370f.

Lines 18–20 were translated in two different versions by Veenhof, AOATT 124 and 377. In the rendition on page 124 he translates "the offer on the market of Kanish is insufficient"; on page 377, "the market of Kanish is not sufficiently supplied." The meaning hangs on whether *maḫīrum* is to be taken as "market" or "market price." We have favored the latter since the first clause dealt with the cost factor.

Lines 21f.— See CAD E 402 (sub 3.) for the expression *ana ūm eṭārim* in the sense "while someone can still be saved."

Line 23 is a bit of a problem owing to its being squeezed onto the left side of the tablet. H. Lewy in her collation notes wrote; *a-šu* plus word divider and translated "I deposited . . ." What appears on the tablet following *mì* is  which I take as LÚ = *awīlum* since LUGAL does not fit our context.

Pa. 30 = L 29–589

1. *a-na A-šùr-na-da*
2. *qí-[bi-]ma um-ma*
3. *A-šur-ta*!*-ak-la-*<*ku-*>*ma*

4. 10 1/2 MA.NA 6 GÍN KÙ.BABBAR
5. *ṣa-ru-⸢pá-⸣am ku-nu-ki-ni*
6. *A-šùr-ma-lik* DUMU *Lá-qí-ip*
7. *na-áš-a-kum ší-tí*
8. AN.NA-*ki-kà ù ší-im*
9. TÚG^{ḫi}-*tí-kà ni-da-ma*
10. *i-šé-pì-a ú-ba-lá-kum*
11. 5 GÚ [AN!.NA]

Edge 12. *Ì-lí-a-lúm*
13. *ú-šé-bi-lam*

Rev. 14. *i-na tí-ir-tí-šu*
15. *um-ma šu-ut-ma*
16. ANŠE$^{ḫi.a}$ *ša A-šùr-na-da*
17. *šé-ri-a-ma*
18. URUDU-*šu li-ší!-ú-ni-im*
19. *ú-mu tám-<kà->ri-šu*
20. *⸢ma-⸣al-ú a-ma-lá*
21. *tí-ir-tí-šu* ANŠE$^{ḫi.a}$
22. *ú-šé-ra-ma* URUDU-*a-kà*
23. *i-sà-ri-du-nim*
24. *a-dí* 10 u_4-*mì ú-za-kà-ma*

Edge 25. *ú-ṣí-a-am*
26. KÙ.BABBAR 1 GÍN *ša ta-kà-nu-ku*
27. *a-mu-ur-ma a-ma-kam*

Left Edge 28. *lá a-sà-ḫu-ur* URUDU-*a-kà*
29. *a-da-ma* KÙ.BABBAR *ú-ba-lá-kum*

Translation of Pa. 30 = L 29–589

(2) Speak (1) to Asshur-nādā. (2) Thus (says) (3) Asshur-taklāku: (6) Asshur-malik son of Lā-qēp (7) is carrying to you (4) 10 1/2 manas (and) 6 shekels of (5) refined (4) silver (5) (bearing) our seals. (9) We will deposit (7) the rest of (8) your tin and the price of (9) your textiles, and (10) I will bring (it) to you in my caravan. (12) Ilī-ālum (13) has sent (11) 5 talents of tin(!) (13) to me.

(15) Thus he said (14) in his report: (17) Release (16) the donkeys of Asshur-nādā (17) and (18) let them carry his copper to me. (19) The time (lit., days) of his merchant (20) has elapsed. According to (21) his report (22) I have released (21) the donkeys (22) and (23) they are loading

(22) your copper. (24) I will be ready to go in 10 days and (25) (then) I will go on my way.

(27) Inspect (26) the silver which you are sealing (down to the last) shekel (27) so there (28) I will not be delayed. (29) I will sell (28) your copper (29) and I will bring the silver to you.

Notes on Pa. 30 = L 29–589

Line 11— A bit of the AN of AN.NA is faintly visible.

Lines 21–23 are rendered by Veenhof AOATT 9 where he takes *ú-šé-ra-ma* as a present of the D stem from *wašārum*. GKT Section 93f in discussing this verb, however, lists all forms with "e" as preterite while the present forms consistently take "a." We have followed GKT in translating the verb "I have released."

Line 26— *Takannakū* > *takannukū* by vowel harmony.

Line 29— *A-da-ma* > *addanma*.

Pa. 31 = L 29–590

1. *um-ma* ^{d}*En-líl-ba-ni-ma*
2. *a-na Áb-Ša-lim*
3. *qí-bi-ma* / 7 GÍN KÙ.BABBAR
4. *du-dí-tam*$_4$ *ku-nu-ki-a*
5. *a-na ṣú-ḫa-ar-tim*
6. *En-na-*ZU.IN *na-ší*
7. *a-ma-kam* 2 *a-ma-tim*
8. *Ud-ru-a-šu* / *ù Ga-da-da*
9. *a-na* É$^{bi\text{-}ti}$*-šu*

Edge 10. *šé-ri-bi-ší-na*

11. *ù ṣú-ḫa-ra-am*

Rev. 12. *ša a-*⌜*šar*⌝ / *Áb-Ša-lim*

13. *ù-ra-bu-ú-ni*
14. *a-na* É$^{bi\text{-}ti}$*-šu*
15. *ta-ru-e-šu* 2$^?$ SÌLA *sà-ar-dam*
16. *le-qé-ma*
17. *ṭá-i-bi-šu* / *a-na* /
18. *ḫa-ra-ni-a* / 5 GÍN KÙ.BABBAR
19. *En-na-*ZU.IN *ir-ší-ma*

20. *ta-ar-bi-it*
21. *ṣú-ḫa-ri-im dí-ni*

Translation of Pa. 31 = L 29–590

(1) Thus (says) Enlil-bāni: (3) Speak (2) to Ab-Shalim, (saying): (6) Enna-Su'en is carrying (3) a 7-shekel silver (4) pectoral (bearing) my seal (5) for (or, to) the young woman. (7) There (10) cause (7) the two women, (8) Udru'ashu and Gadada, (10) to enter (9) his house.

(11) Furthermore, (15) return (14) to his house (11) the lad (12) whom Ab-Shalim (13) reared. (16) Take (15) a 2(?)-*qa* load (16) and (17) bring the matter (it) to a happy conclusion. (19) Enna-Su'en has earned (18) 5 shekels of silver (17) for (participating in) (18) my caravan, (19) and (so) (21) pay (20) the fee for rearing (21) the lad.

Notes on Pa. 31 = L 29–590

Line 2— For the PN Ab-Shalim, see the discussion of line 10 below.

Line 8— The feminine PN Udru'ašu appears also in BIN 4, 68:15 in the form *Ud-ru-wa-šu*. The feminine PN *Ga-da-da* occurs in ICK 1, 172:3.

Line 10— From the following considerations we learn that Ab-Šalim was a female business associate of Enlil-bāni's and that the feminine imperative (*šēribīšina*) is, therefore, proper. From the nature and meaning of the name Ab-Šalim, "Šalim (is divine) Father" or "The (divine) Father makes well," we cannot discern the sex of its bearer. In the form Abu-Šalim, the PN occurred frequently in OA times for males. But in BIN 4, 68 feminine possessive pronouns repeatedly appear referring to the addressee, Ab-Šalim. TTC 19, a letter of Asshur-lamassī to Ab-Šalim, clearly shows the recipient to be female. For example, line 9 has *a-ḫa-tí a-tí*, line 8 has *na-áš-a-ki-im*. Likewise, KTS 2a was written to a certain Ab-Šalim to whom the dative pronoun *kim* is referred in lines 9 and 14. CCT 4, 13b is also a letter from Enlil-bāni to Ab-Šalim in which Ab-Šalim is the antecedent of the feminine pronoun suffixes, *ki* or *kim*, in lines 13, 21, 23, and 25. ATHE 24 (Tablet and Case) concerns, among others, the *gubabtum*-priestess, Ab-Šalim daughter of Amur-Ištar. We cannot determine what the relationship between Enlil-bāni and Ab-Šalim was, but it is clear from out text, CCT 4, 13b; BIN 4, 68; and BIN 6, 69 that she handled significant affairs for Enlil-bāni. Larsen (OACP 16, n. 13) opined that she was his wife, but at this point we cannot make a final judgment.

Line 12— Collation shows that *šar* is fairly well preserved. *Ša ašar* . . . is unusual.

Line 15— See AHw 1029a for *sardum*, a verbal adjective from *sarādum*, "to load."

Lines 17–19— The form *ir-ší-ma* may be taken two ways: 1) *irši*, a G preterite from *rašā'um*, "to get, earn" (see AHw 961f.) or 2) *eršī*, a G imperative, feminine, singular from *erāšum*, "to ask, request, desire." It is difficult to know which proposal to favor here since the verb *erāšum* may take a double object, "to request something (from) someone." The second possibility would be translated: "[(19)] Request [(18)] 5 shekels of silver [(19)] (from) Enna-Su'en [(17)] for [(18)] my caravan!" or "when (at) my caravan (arrives)!"

Line 20— For *tarbītum*, "money for rearing a child," see GKT Section 55e and ICK 1, 32:24.

Pa. 32 = L 29-591

1. IGI *Ú-sà-nim*
2. *ù Ú-zu-a* DUMU *A-bi-a-a*
3. *ni-kà-sí*
4. *ni-sí-ma*
5. 5/6 MA.NA AN.NA
6. *i-li-bi Ku-ra*
7. *A-mur-*DINGIR *i-dì*
8. 6 *ku-ta-ni*

Edge 9. *ša Ku-ra* <*ša*> *iš-ti*

Rev. 10. *A-mur-*DINGIR *i-ba-ší-ú*

11. *e-zi-ib* 1/3 MA.NA
12. KÙ.BABBAR *ša i-na a-lim*[ki]
13. *ḫa-bu-lu-ma i-na*
14. *Kà-ni-iš i-na*
15. *e-ra-bi-šu-ma i-ša-qú-lu*
16. *ù bé-ú-lá-tù-šu*
17. *i-na li-bi-šu-ma*

Translation of Pa. 32 = L 29–591

(1) In the presence of Usānum (2) and Uzu'a son of Abiā (4) we settled (3) accounts, (4) and (we determined that) (7) Amur-ilī has deposited (5) 5/6 of a mana of tin (6) in Kura's account. (11) He left (8) 6 cloths (9) belonging to Kura which (10) are (9) with (10) Amur-ilī. (17) In his account there is (11) 1/3 of a mana of (12) silver which (13) he owed in (14) the City (of Assur) (13) and (which) (15) he will weigh out (13) in (14) Kanish when (15) he arrives; (16) also his investment capital is in his own account.

Notes on Pa. 32 = L 29–591

Lines 1–4— In other reports of this kind, a court is called into session for the settling of accounts and sometimes the settlement was accomplished before the sacred dagger of Asshur. The two gentlemen of these lines were apparently judges or perhaps agents of the Mercantile Center (*kārum*).

Lines 3f.— *Nikkassī šasā'um* = "to settle accounts." See AOATT 435 and AHw 789a.

Line 8— Collation verifies that the number is 6, not 5.

Lines 9–11 are troublesome due to the ambiquity involved in the form *e-zi-ib* of line 11. *E-zi-ib* has six possible renderings: 1) "I left," 2) "I will leave," 3) "he left," 4) "he will leave," 5) "leave!" and 6) "besides" (GKT Section 102j, CAD E 429a, and AHw 270a). If we select possibility 3) to make this clause parallel the one preceding, we may interpolate *ša* in line 9. If, on the other hand, we consider number 6), we also get reasonable sense: (17) In his account are (8) 6 cloths (9) of Kura's which (10) are (9) with (10) Amur-ilī (11) not to mention the 1/3 of a mana (12) (of) silver which (13) he owes (12) in the City (of Assur) (13) and (which) (15) he will weigh out (13) in (14) Kanish when (15) he arrives, (16) and also his investment capital.

Line 13— Which of the two business associates is the subject of the verbs, *ḫabulu* and *išaqqulu*, is hard to determine.

Pa. 33 = L 29–592

1. *a-na Pu-šu-ki-in*
2. *qí-bi-ma um-ma I-dí-Ku-*[*bu-ma*]

3. *i-na u_4-mì-im*
4. *ša ú-nu-tù-um i-⸢na⸣*
5. É.GAL-*lim ú-ṣí-a-ni*
6. *iš-tí / a-li-ki-im*
7. *pá-ni-im-ma ú-nu-tí*
8. *áb-kà-am a-bi a-ta*
9. *be-lí a-ta i-ḫi-da*
10. *a-na ma-nim*

Edge 11. *lá-tí-ki-il_5*

Rev. 12. KÙ.BABBAR / *ší-im* ⸢AN.⸣NA-⸢*ki-*⸣*kà*
13. *lu ú-šé-bi_4-lá-[ku-]ni*
14. *A-šur ú il_5-kà*
15. *li-ṭù-lá šu-ma*
16. *a-dí-ni / al*[!]*-qí i-na*
17. *ra-mì-ni-a / lu a-dí*
18. *lá-ma / ša-ri-im*
19. *ú-ša-ba-ni / lu-qú-tí*
20. *áb-kà-am ù a-nu-ku*

Edge 21. *a-wa-at-kà*
22. *ša-ma-am*

Left Edge 23. *a-li-e i-ḫi-id*

Translation of Pa. 33 = L 29–592

(2) Speak (1) to Pūshu-kēn. (2) Thus (says) Īdī-Kubum: (8) Dispatch to me (7) my equipment (6) with the (7) first (6) messenger (3) on the (very) day (4) that the equipment (5) is released (lit., goes out) (4) from (5) the palace. (8) You (are) my father; you (are) (9) my boss (master). Take heed! (10) Whom (11) may I trust? (13) I verily sent to you (12) the silver (for) the price of your tin. (15) May (14) Asshur and your god (15) take note! If (16) I had already received (it), (17) verily I would have deposited (it) (16) in (17) my own account. (19) I will pay (it) in full (18) before the King; (so) (20) dispatch (19) my goods (20) to me! Then I (23) will be able (22) to hear (21) your case (word). (23) Take heed!

Notes on Pa. 33 = L 29–592

Lines 4, 7, and 19— Note that *unūtum* interchanges with *luqūtum*. See Larsen, OACP 86 (note on l. 11), where he suggests "goods" for *unūtum* when used in this circumstance.

Line 9— We may take *i-ḫi-da* as imperative plus ventive from *naḫādum* or as a scribal error for *i-ḫi-id*. Collation shows *da*, not *id*.

Line 11— *Lá-tí-ki-*il_5 = *lū atikkil* (GKT Section 77a). For the expression, *ana mannim latikkil*, "whom else should I trust?" see GKT Section 84b where TC 1, 6:3–5 is cited as an example.

Line 12— The *ki* is not clear on the text, but likely.

Line 13— *Lū ušēbilakunni.* Hecker notes (GKT Section 132a) in OA the "positive assertive oath" may be expressed by *lū* plus the subjunctive preterite.

Line 16— For *adīni* ("until now, already" with positive verb and "not yet" with negated verb), see especially GKT Section 137c.

According to collation the *al* is strange,  .

Line 18— *Lāma* ("before") may be used either as conjunction or preposition. See GKT Sections 103g and 155.

Šarrum, "king," spelled phonetically appears rarely in OA. See Balkan TTKY VII/31a, where he published the valuable text g/t 35; the form *ša-ra-né-e* appears in lines 10 and 14. The phonetic spelling also occurs in TC 2, 54:17 (see J. Lewy HUCA 27 [1956] 14, n. 64).

Line 19— Collation shows that the third sign is a little damaged. It could be *ma*, but the indentation at the front of the sign appears to be an irregularity in the clay rather than a vertical wedge. We, therefore, prefer *ú-ša-ba-ni*.

Line 22— *Ša-ma-am* = *šamâm*, G infinitive of *šamā'um*; see GKT Section 95e.

Pa. 34 = L 29–593

1′. 5 TÚG *I-na-aḫ-*[DINGIR$^{?}$]
2′. 11 TÚG *Pí-lá-aḫ-Ištar*
3′. *ù Kà-wi-a*
4′. [x] TÚG$^{!}$ *Ša-lim-A-šùr* DUMU *I-*[ ]
5′. [*A-*]*šùr* [ ]
Rev. 1″. 5$^{!}$ TÚG *I*[ ]
2″. 10 TÚG *I-dí-Ku-bu-*[*um*]
3″. 5 TÚG *A-šùr-ma-lik* DUMU *A-šùr-ba-ni*
4″. 5 TÚG *Bu-zu-ta-a*
Edge 5″. 5 TÚG *E-na*[ ]
(end of tablet)

Translation of Pa. 34 = L29–593

(1′) 5 textiles, Inaḫ-[ilī(?)]. (2′) 11 textiles, Pilaḫ-Ishtar (3′) and Kawia. (4′) x textiles, Shalim-Asshur son of I[ ]. (5′) [As]shur [ ].

(1″) 5(!) textiles, I[ ]. (2″) 10 textiles, Īdī-Kub[um]. (3″) 5 textiles, Asshur-malik son of Asshur-bāni. (4″) 5 textiles, Buzutā. (5″) 5 textiles, Enna-[ ]. (end of tablet)

Notes on Pa. 34 = L 29–593

Only the upper part of the tablet remains. Collation adds nothing to understanding this text.

All the PNs are attested elsewhere in OA.

Pa. 35 = L 29–595

Edge 1′. [*a-*]*lim*^{ki} URUDU *ma-dam*
2′. [ ] *e mu du* [ ]
Rev. 3′. [ ] *ma-ma*$^{?}$-[*an*$^{?}$]
4′. [ ] *iš šu* [ ]
5′. [*li-*]*li-kam* / *a-ma-kam* ⌜*ra*$^{?}$*-dí*$^{?}$⌝
6′. *Šu-Be-lúm* / *me-et* x x x [ ]
7′. *ḫu-lu-qá-e-a* / *tam-kà-ru-*[*um*$^{?}$]
8′. *lá i-ṣa-bu-tù-ni* / *ḫu-*[*lu-qá-e-a*$^{?}$]
9′. *ša-am* / *šu-up-ra-ma ṭup-*[*pá-am*$^{?}$]
10′. *ša ku-nu-ki-a lá-dí-in*$^{!}$ [ ]
(end lost)

Translation of Pa. 35 = L 29–595

(1′) the City (of Assur), much copper (2′) (?) (3′) who(ever)(?) (4′) (?) (5′) let it come(?). Bring (it)(?) there. (6′) Shu-Bēlum is dead. [ ] (7′) The merchant(?) (8′) will not seize (7′) my lost merchandise. (9′) Buy (something in place of) (8′) [my lost merchandise(?).] (9′) Write me and (10′) let me give (9′) a tab[let] (10′) (bearing) my seal. (end lost)

Notes on Pa. 35 = L 29–595

The preserved portion of this text begins at the bottom edge of the obverse and continues onto the top part of the reverse.

Line 2′— Probably one sign is missing at the beginning of the line.

Line 3′— Two signs are gone from the beginning of the line.

Line 5′— The reading of the last two signs is tentative.

Line 6′— I cannot make anything of the last three visible signs. They look like either UR BA BA or UR MA MA.

Line 10′— Collation shows that the *in* is likely, though not completely sure.

Lá-di-in = *lū+addin*.

Pa. 36 = L 29–596

1. x GÚ 13 MA.NA URUDU
2. SIG_5 *Ḫa-bu-ra-ta-i-um*
3. *ša-bu-ru-um*
4. *i-ṣé-er A-šùr-ma-lik*
5. DUMU *Ta-ku-a*
6. ZU-*i-dá-dá i-šu*
7. *iš-tù ḫa-mu-uš-tim*
8. *ša Šu-*^{d}*En-líl*
9. *ù E-lá-lí*

Rev. 10. *a-na ku-bu-ur*
11. *ú-ṭí-tim i-ša-qal*
12. *šu-ma i-na ú-mì-šu*
13. *ma-al*$^{!}$*-ú-tim lá ìš-qúl*
14. *i-na* ITI 1 KAM *a-na*
15. 10 MA.NA-*im* / [[x]]
16. 1 MA.NA TA URUDU
17. *ú-ṣa-áb*
18. IGI *Bu-zu-li-a*
19. [ ]-bi_4-*im*

Translation of Pa. 36 = L 29–596

(6) Zu'idada has (a debt of) (1) x talents (and) 13 manas of (2) good-quality, (3) broken up Ḫaburatean (1) copper (4) against Asshur-malik

(5) son of Taku'a. (11) He will weigh (it) out (counting) (7) from the *ḫamushtum*-period (8) of Shū-Enlil (9) and Elāli (10) to the ripening of (11) the grain. (12) If (13) he does not weigh (it) out (12) within the (13) full amount (12) of his allotted time, (17) he shall pay an additional (16) mana of copper (14) per (15) 10 manas. (18) In the presence of Buzulia, (19) [ ]bim.

Notes on Pa. 36 = L 29–596

Line 1— Collation verifies that the number is entirely lost.

Lines 1–3— Haburatean copper is known from VAT 9231:5ff. and TC 1, 55:5, 18, both rendered by J. Lewy in EL I p. 134, n. a. See Veenhof AOATT 241 (also n. 373) for the possible location of Haburatum in the "Habur triangle." J. Lewy (JAOS 78 [1958] 94), on the other hand, identified the copper-producing Haburat with classical Cabira in Pontus, modern Niskar; see also KTBl p. 24. J. Lewy (Mélanges I. Levy [1953] 298, n. 5 and OrNS 21 [1952] 265–271), however, recognized a *Ḫa-bu-ra* which lay on the Habur River. We apparently have two places with similar names: *Ḫa-bu-ra* on the Habur River, and copper-producing Haburat in Pontus.

Line 5— The PN *Ta-ku-a* is unknown to me elsewhere. The vertical stroke shown in Mrs. Lewy's drawing is present on the text.

Line 6— The rare PN *Śu-e-ta-ta* was treated by J. Lewy in EL I p. 38, n. b, where he suggested that this spelling stood for *Sú-e-(en)-dá-dá*, "Sin (is) uncle." No one else has taken up the suggestion. At that time Lewy knew only two occurrences, EL 48:x + 3 (= Gol. 9 = KTK 83) and 258:1 (= BIN 4, 100). We may add now ATHE 3:3; 34:24; ICK 2, 11:B 6; 345:3 (ZU-*i-dá-dá*) and CCT 6, 1b:3, as well as our text with the spelling which seems to follow ICK 2, 354:3.

Lines 10f.— For *kubur uṭṭitim*, "the ripening of the grain," see CAD K 484b.

Line 13— The *al* of *mal'uttum* is strangely written.

Line 15— Collation shows the word divider followed by what looks like an erased sign.

Pa. 37 = L 29–600

1. IGI *I-ku-nim* // DUMU ^{d}UTU-*ba-ni*
2. IGI *A-šùr-iš-tí-kál*
3. DUMU *Ḫi-na-a* IGI *Ú-ṣur-ša-A-šùr*

4. DUMU *A-šùr-ša-du-ni*
5. *ta-ma-lá-gu*$_5$ *ša Lu-zi-na*
6. *ša A-mur-Ištar* DUMU *Šu-Ištar*
7. *ú Šu-A-nim* DUMU *Me-na-nim*
8. *a-na Áb-Ša-lim*
9. *e*$^!$*-zi-bu-ni* / *ta-ma-lá-gi*$_5$
10. *A-šùr-*GAL *ú-šé-ṣí-a-ma*

Edge 11. *ta-ma-lá-gi*$_5$
12. *ni-ip-ṭur*$_4$*-ma*

Rev. 13. *mì-ma* KÙ.BABBAR *lá i-ba-ší*
14. *ku-nu-ki ša pá-ni*
15. *ta-ma-lá-gi*$_5$*-<a>* / *ni-iš-ku-um-ma*
16. *ni-ik-≪ku-≫nu-uk-ma*
17. *a-na Šál-me-ḫi-im*
18. DUMU *Lu-zi-na*
19. *ni-dí-in*

Translation of Pa. 37 = L 29–600

(1) In the presence of Ikūnum son of Shamash-bāni, (2) in the presence of Asshurish-tikal (3) son of Ḫinnā, in the presence of Uṣur-sha-Asshur (4) son of Asshur-shadûni. (5) (In regard to) the containers of Luzina (6) which Amur-Ishtar son of Shū-Ishtar (7) and Shū-Anum son of Menanum (9) left (8) for Ab-Shalim — (10) Asshur-rabi brought out (9) (those) containers and (12) we unpacked (11) (those) containers (12) and (13) there was no silver whatever (in them). (15) We have (re-)placed (14) seals on the exterior of (15) (those) containers and (16) we have (thus) sealed (them) and (19) we have given (them) (17) to Shal(i)m-aḫum (18) son of Luzina.

Notes on Pa. 37 = L 29–600

Line 1— The text contains two vertical wedges between Ikūnum and DUMU with no apparent meaning beyond dividing the words.

Line 4— The PN *A-šùr-ša-du-ni* appears only in one other OA document so far as I know, CCT 4, 40b + 41a:4. Stephens PNC 93b traced the last element to *šadû*, "mountain." See Tallqvist APN 307b for some later PNs which make use of *šadûni*, "DN is our mountain."

Lines 5, 9, 11, and 15— On *tamalagum*, "coffer, box, trunk," see J. Lewy OrNS 19 (1950) 2–7, where he also documented *šinīšu tamalagū* ("double boxes") and *šalāšīšu tamalagū* ("triple boxes").

Line 9— The *e* is squeezed at the very edge of the tablet.

Line 17— Our treatment of the PN follows J. Lewy EL II p. 184.

Pa. 38 = L 29–601

1. 1 *na-ru-uq* 2 DUG
2. *ar-ša-tim a-na* DAM
3. DINGIR-*na-da a-dí-in*
4. 3 DUG *a-na ḫa-mu-uš-tim*
5. *i-dí-nu* 2 DUG *a-na* É
6. *A-šùr-ták-lá-ku*
7. *ša ḫa-bu-lá-ni-ni*
8. *nu-ta-er* 2 DUG
9. *ša ma-zi-tim*

Edge 10. 2 DUG *ša ta-pá-lá-tim*

Rev. 11. *i-dí-nu* 1 DUG

12. *a-na nu-a-ri-im*
13. *a-dí-in*
14. 1 DUG *ša-ar-ša-ra-nam*
15. *a-ma-ar-nu-a-tim*
16. *i-dí-nu*
17. *ša-ar-ša-ra-nùm*
18. *ar-ša-tum*

Edge 19. *i-ri-ḫa*

Translation of Pa. 38 = L 29–601

(3) I have given (1) 1 sack (and) 2 pots of (2) barley to the wife of (3) Ilī-nādā. (5) They gave (4) 3 pots to the *ḫamushtum*-official. (8) We returned (5) to the house of (6) Asshur-taklāku (5) the 2 pots (7) which we owed. (11) They have given (8) 2 pots (9) of "pressed beer" (and) (10) 2 pots of *tapalātum*-beer. (13) I gave (11) 1 pot (12) to the musician. (16) They gave (14) 1 pot (and) a half-pot (15) of barley beer(?). (17) A half-pot (of) (18) barley (19) is left over.

Notes on Pa. 38 = L 29–601

Pa. 38 = L 29–601 was offered in transliteration only by H. Lewy RSO 39 (1964) 191, n.1.

Lines 1, 4, 5, 8, 10, 11, and 14— On the OA measurements of capacity, see H. Lewy RSO 39 (1964) 190–197, where she showed the following ratios:

naruqqum	1		
karpatum (= *ṣimdum*)	4	1	
šaršarānum	8	2	1
qa	120	30	15

Line 2— While taking *aršātum* as "wheat(?)" on the basis of the broader Mesopotamian usage, the CAD (A_2 308) allows the possibility that *aršātum* = GIG may refer to some form of barley and cites H. Lewy JAOS 76 (1956) 201, n. 1, for this view. AHw 71b simply takes *aršātum* as "barley." See Pa. 47:7 below for *naruq* GIG.

Line 4— *Ḫamuštum* here designates a person rather than the *ḫamuštum*-period. *Ḫamuštum* might also stand for *ḫamištum*, "committee of five." See Larsen's comment in OACC 384.

Line 9— AHw 637b takes *ma-zi-tim* from *mazi'um*, a verbal adjective from *mazā'um*, "to squeeze out." The other associations of this word suggest that it describes some type of beer.

Line 10— This expression x DUG *ša ta-pá-lá-tim* appears also in KTH 35:10 and 18, a document similar in content to Pa. 38. J. Lewy had no suggestion to offer beyond the possible association of the word with the verb *tabālum*. Other occurrences appear in VAT 13517:7f. (*qé-ma-am ša ta-pá-lá-tim*; see KTH, p. 46); CCT 5, 33a:21f. (*mì-iš-lu-um ta-pá-lá-tum*); and CCT 6, 40a:3–5 (4 *na-ru-uq* [4]*ar-ša-tim* [5]*ta-pá-lá-tim*). Thus this commodity may be measured by "halves" and in "pots." The description in VAT 13517 forces us to modify von Soden's (AHw 1296f.) evaluation that the term designates "good beer." Since CCT 6, 40a associates *tapalātum* with barley and since the other commodities in our text are made from barley, we have arbitrarily translated this term as "beer" with reservation.

Line 12— *Nu-a-ri-im* is taken by AHw 748f. as "musician." See also Hirsch UAR 58b who lists ICK 1, 156:14; Gelb 59:32; and TC 3, 168:12 as examples.

Lines 14 and 17— For *šaršarānum*, see the note above on line 1.

Line 15— AHw 612a cites the occurrences of *marnu'ātum* and suggests the meaning "eine Mehlspeise." One might also think of some form of barley beer as a possible meaning for the term.

Pa. 39 = L 29–602

1. *um-ma A-šur-i-dí-ma*
2. *a-na A-šur-na-da*
3. *qí-bi*$_4$*-ma* 5 GÍN KÙ.BABBAR
4. *i-na e-ra-bi*$_4$*-šu-ma*
5. *Ás-qú-dí-a ša-áš-qí-il*$_5$*-ma*
6. *iš-tí ší-im*

Edge 7. ANŠE *ku-nu-uk-ma*

Rev. 8. *i-pá-ni-e-ma*

9. *šé-bi*$_4$*-lam*
10. 1 ^{túg}*ku-ta-nu-um*
11. *i-ṭù-pì-a*
12. *lá lá-pì-it*
13. *ša A-šur-ta-ak-lá-ku*

Edge 14. *Ás-qú-dí-a-ma*

Left Edge 15. *na-áš-a-kum*

Translation of Pa. 39 = L 29–602

(1) Thus (says) Asshur-īdī. (3) Speak (2) to Asshur-nādā. (5) Cause Asqudia to weigh out (3) 5 shekels of silver (4) when he comes in, (5) and (7) seal (it) (6) together with the price of (7) the donkey, and (9) send (it) to me (8) as soon as possible. (12) Not (10) one cloth (12) is to be entered (11) on my tablet. (14) Asqudia (15) is carrying to you (13) what belongs to Asshur-taklāku.

Notes on Pa. 39 = L 29–602

Line 2— Collation shows that the *a* at the beginning of the line is clear.

Line 3— Collation verifies that KÙ.BABBAR is there but is squeezed onto the edge. The BABBAR is stretched out and faint.

Lines 5 and 14— The PN *Ás-qú-dí-a* is rare appearing in KUG 27:14 (also a letter of Asshur-īdī to Asshur-nādā); CCT 5, 18d:11; and BIN 4, 79:4 (broken context). Whether this PN is to be associated with the more common Asqudum is doubtful.

Line 11— Collation shows that the *i* is inscribed over another sign. The DU is strangely written but clear; it is not *ṭup*.

Line 13— The *ak* is squeezed but clear.

Pa. 40 A = L 29–603 Inner Tablet

	1. 10 1/2 GÍN KÙ.BABBAR
	2. *i-ṣé-er*
	3. *Ba-ru-ki-in*
	4. *ú a-ší-ti-šu*
	5. *Nu-ùḫ-⸢ší-⸣tim*
	6. *Na-ki-li-e-ed*
	7. GAL *ša-qé-e*
Edge	8. *i-šu*
Rev.	9. KÙ.BABBAR
	10. *a-na* ITI 11 KAM
	11. *i-ša-qú-lu*
	12. *šu-ma lá i-ša-qú-lu*
	13. 1 1/2 GÍN TA KÙ.BABBAR
	14. *i-na* ITI 1 KAM
	15. *ṣí-ib-tám*
Edge	16. ⸢*ú-*⸣*ṣú-bu*
Left Edge	17. IGI *Zi-ra-bi*
	18. IGI *Ni-wa-aḫ-šu*
	19. IGI *A-lá-ri-a*

Pa. 40 B = L 29–603 Case

	1. KIŠIB *Zi-ra-bi*
	2. KIŠIB *Ni-wa-aḫ-šu*
	3. KIŠIB *A-lá-ri-a*
	4. KIŠIB *Ba-ru-ki-in*
	5. KIŠIB *Nu*!*-ùḫ-ší-*[*tim*]
	6. *a-ší-ti-šu*
	7. 10 1/2 ⸢GÍN⸣ KÙ.BABBAR
Rev.	8. ⸢*a-*⸣*na* ITI 10 KAM
	9. *i-ša-qú-lu šu-ma*
	10. *lá i-ša-qal*
Left Edge	11. [1 1/2 G]ÍN KÙ.BABBAR
	12. [*i-na* ITI] 1 KAM
	13. [*ṣí-ib-t*]*ám ú-ṣú-bu*

Translation of Pa. 40 A = L 29–603 Tablet

(6) Nakilēd, (7) the Chief Cupbearer, (8) has (a debt of) (1) 10 1/2 shekels of silver (2) against (3) Barukin (4) and his wife, (6) Nuḫshitum.

(11) They will weigh out (9) the silver (10) within 11 months. (12) If they do not weigh out (the silver by then), (16) they shall add (13) 1 1/2 shekels of silver (per mana) (14) per month as (15) interest. (17) In the presence of Zirabi, (18) in the presence of Niwaḫshu, (19) (and) in the presence of Alaria.

Translation of Pa. 40 B = L 29–603 Case

(1) The seal of Zirabi. (2) The seal of Niwaḫshu. (3) The seal of Alaria. (4) The seal of Barukin. (5) The seal of Nuḫshitum, (6) his wife.

(9) They shall weigh out (7) 10 1/2 shekels of silver (8) within 10(!) months. (9) If (10) he(!) does not weigh (it) out (on time), (13) they shall add (11) [1 1/2 she]kels of silver (per mana) (12) [per mo]nth (13) [as inter]est.

Notes on Pa. 40 A = L 29–603 Tablet

Line 3— The PN *Ba-ru-ki-in* is known from TC 3, 218:A 13 and B 1 as a witness. Whether the rare PN *Bu-ur-qá-num* (ICK 1, 57:13[!]; ICK 2, 152:x + 11; and Kennedy and Garelli JCS 14 [1960] 11:37) or *Ba-ru-kà* (CCT 1, 41b:10) should be related to Barukin is impossible to say.

Line 5— The feminine PN occurs in BIN 6, 104:2 as the recipient of a letter from Puzur-Asshur referring to her father, but not to her husband. The similar feminine PN, *Nu-ḫu-ša-tám*, occurs in BIN 4, 186:A 10 and B 11.

Lines 6f.— The PN is known from some dozen OA documents; see Kennedy and Garelli JCS 14 (1960) 19 and Garelli AC 144. Nowhere else is the title *rab šāqê* applied to Nakilēd, although there is a Nakilēd, *rab šarīkē*, mentioned in EL 5:4 (= TCL 1, 242) as witnessing the document. Lewy translated this term as "Obersten der Tempelsklaven" without note. GKT Section 54c renders *šarīkum* as "Oblate, Tempelsklave" and refers to Hirsch UAR 58, n. 301, for further references. See also ICK 1, 139:10.

The title *rab šāqê* also appears in TMH 4b (= Jena 441) just after a break: (12) *qí-bi*$_4$*-ma i-na* É.*bi*$_4$ [x] (13) GAL *ša-qé-e* 6 GÍN KÙ.BABBAR (14) ≪KÙ.BABBAR≫ *ḫa-bu-lu-nim* . . . The *rab šāqê* official is not named, nor is Nakilēd mentioned in the preserved portions of the text.

Line 10— Collation verifies the numeral 11 although the case clearly has 10.

Lines 17–19— Mrs. Lewy's published line drawings inadvertently omitted these lines from the left edge of the Tablet although they are included in her collation notes.

Alaria appears in ICK 1, 19:A 4 and B 26 as the father of Šakri'uman.

Niwaḫšu occurs in KTK 92:x + 16; Niwaḫšušar in TC 1, 33:15 and TCL 1, 240:21. *Ni-ma-aḫ-šu* in CCT 1, 41b:6 is probably the same PN with "w" and "m" interchanging. *Ni-wa-šu* in TC 1, 68:2 may be either a variant of Niwaḫšu or a scribal error.

I cannot find *Zi-ra-bi* anywhere.

Notes on Pa. 40 B = L 29–603 Case

The case shows a partial seal impression with two partial lines of writing both of which begin with DINGIR with nothing else preserved.

Line 10— The scribe seemingly forgot the wife in writing *išaqqal* instead of *išaqqulu*. Compare line 12 of the Tablet.

Lines 8–10 are located on the bottom of the Reverse.

Pa. 41 = L 29–604

1. *um-ma* DAM.GÀR-*ru-um-ma*
2. *a-na Bu-zu* / *qí-bi-ma*
3. *a-ḫi a-ta* / *a-na-kam*
4. *e-ma-ra-am* / *a-dí-na-ku-ma*
5. *e-ma-ru-um* / *eq-lam*
6. *a-šu-mì* / *tám-kà-ri-im*
7. *e-ti-iq* / *a-ḫi a-ta*
8. *a-wi-il*$_5$ / *gi*$_5$*-mì-li-im*
9. *a-na-ku* / *a-ma-kam*
10. *i-na ší-im e-ma-ri-im*

Edge 11. 5[!] GÍN KÙ.BABBAR

12. *a-šar ša-ḫu-za-tí-ni*

Rev. 13. *dí-in* / *a-na ší-tí* KÙ.BABBAR

14. *ší-ma-am* / *li-qí-a-ma*
15. *šé-bi*$_4$*-lam* / *a-ḫa* 1 GÍN
16. KÙ.BABBAR / *ša am-tim*
17. *tù-kà-al* SÍG$^{hi.a}$
18. 5 MA.NA *lu-bu-ší-ša*
19. *šé-bi*$_4$*-lam* / *a-na ṣú-ùḫ-ri-im*

20. *lá ta-ra-ší*
21. *ki-ma / ša <i-na> ša-ḫa-tí-kà*
22. *wa-áš-bu / lá ta-ra-ší*

Translation of Pa. 41 = L 29–604

(1) Thus (says) the merchant. (2) Speak to Buzu, (saying): (3) You (are) my brother. Here (4) I gave you a donkey, and (5) the donkey (7) has crossed (5) the country (6) in the merchant's name. (7) You (are) my brother. (9) I (am) (8) a man (in a position to do you) a favor. (9) There (13) give (11) 5(!) shekels of silver (10) from the price of the donkey (12) wherever you have been instructed. (14) Make a purchase for me (13) for the rest of the silver, (14) and send (it) to me.

(15) Besides (or, another matter): (17) you are holding (15) one shekel of (16) silver belonging to the maid. (19) Send to me (18) 5 manas (17) of wool, (18) her clothing (allowance). (20) You must not trouble yourself (19) about the little one. (22) You must not be troubled (21) as (you would) with the one who (22) was residing (21) with you.

Notes on Pa. 41 = L 29–604

Line 2— The PN *Bu-zu* is attested in CCT 3, 30:33. *Bu-zi* in Gol. 20:2 (= KTK 19) may be the same PN. Of course, one may consider PNs which begin with *buzu*: *Bu-zu-ta*, *Bu-zu-a*, *Bu-zu-zu*, *Bu-zu-li-a*, and *Bu-zu-zi-im*.

Line 8— For the expression *awīl gimillim anāku*, see CAD G 74a.

Lines 11–15 are treated by Veenhof (AOATT 371) who was probably right to read the numeral 5 in line 11 as shown by collation. The last wedge on the right top is barely visible.

Line 15— The expression *a-ḫa* is unique. *Aḫamma* ("together with") does not fit the context well, nor does *a-ḫa a-ḫa* (GKT Section 61g) in the sense of "side by side," "here and there," or "one by one." The context favors some meaning like "by the way, besides, another matter."

Line 17— Veenhof discusses the wool trade in AOATT 130–139.

Lines 18f. are rendered by Veenhof in AOATT 90, n. 143, where he explains why *lubūšiša* must mean "her clothing allowance."

Line 19— The *na* of *ana* is correct according to collation.

Line 21— It may not be necessary to insert *ina* for the meaning we derive from this sentence. *Kīma* and *ša* occasionally occur together.

Pa. 42 = L 29–606

1. *um-ma Wa-al-ḫa-áš-na-ma*
2. *a-na Ku-na-ni*$^{!}$*-a*
3. *qí-bi*$_4$*-ma* / *mì-šu-um*
4. *ta-ra-ší-i*
5. *a-na-ku* / *ba-al-ṭá-ku-ma*
6. *a-tí-i*
7. *ta-ra-ší-i*

Edge 8. *a-na A-šur-e-na-am*

Rev. 9. *qí-bi*$_4$*-ma* [[*bi*]]

10. *iš-ra-am* /
11. *ú ša-ḫi-ri-in*
12. *ú ša-am-nam*
13. *ú-šé-bi*$_4$*-lá-kum*
14. *e-mì* / *a-ta*
15. *šu-ma a-ḫa-tí*

Edge 16. *té-zi-ib*

Left Edge 17. *ša e-pu-šu-kà*

18. *ta-mar*

Translation of Pa. 42 = L 29–606

(1) Thus (says) Walḫashna. (3) Speak (2) to Kunania, (saying): (3) Why (4) are you troubled? (5) I am in good health, but (6) you (7) are troubled!

(9) Speak (8) to Asshur-ennam, (saying): (13) I sent to you (10) a belt (11) and a pair of shoe clasps (12) and oil. (14) You (are) my brother-in-law. (15) If you (16) desert (or, divorce) (15) my sister, (18) you shall see (17) what I make (of) you!

Notes on Pa. 42 = L 29–606

This short letter is tantalizing, to say the least. The relationship of the three persons involved in this letter is complicated by lack of data.

Walḫašna and Asshur-ennam clearly are males related by marriage; Kunania is a female whose relationship (if any) to the men is unclear. If she is the sister of line 15, we can conclude that Walḫašna was her brother and Asshur-ennam, her husband. If this deduction is correct, *emum* of line 14 would then mean "brother-in-law" in addition to "father-in-law" and "son-in-law" (see AHw 215b and CAD E 154–156). Unfortunately this deduction is unprovable at the present.

Line 1— The masculine PN *Wa-al-ḫa-áš-na* is unknown to me elsewhere in this form. Similar PNs appear only occasionally: *Wa-lá-aḫ-ší-na*, EL 107:A 3, B 3, 8 (= KTS 46); *Wa-al-aḫ'-šu*, ICK 1, 123:19; *Wa-al-ḫi-iš*, ICK 1, 190:25 (also AC 148), and *Wa-al-ḫi-iš-na*, ICK 2, 127:x + 29. The PN *Wal-aḫši-na* is listed in Bilgiç "Ortsnamen" AfO 15 (1945–51) 5 (sub 3).

Line 2— The feminine PN *Ku-na-ni-a* is better known: BIN 4, 183:5 (= EL 214); BIN 6, 1:2; 17:1; 84:3 (*A-šur-e-n*[*a-am*] appears in line 8); CCT 4, 21a:2, 4 (a letter of *En-nam-A-šùr* to *Ku-na-ni-a*); CCT 6, 7b:3; EL 158:16 (= TC 2, 72) as witness; ICK 1, 112:15; KTBl 5:2 (*Ku-na-ni-a* was a recipient along with *En-um-A-šur* and others); KTH 5:2; 6:2; and TTC 26:4.

The *ni* of the PN was poorly written by the scribe.

Line 10— See Veenhof's discussion of *išrum* in AOATT 176–178. Collation shows that there is a word divider following *išram*.

Line 13— Collation shows a poorly inscribed *šé*.

Line 15— I take the word *a-ḫa-tí* as the substantive "my sister" since the feminine PN, Aḫatum, always appears with mimation.

Pa. 43 = L 29–607

1. ⸢*um-*⸣*ma A-šur-*GAL*-ma*
2. *a-na* ⸢*Ḫa-*⸣*tí-tim*
3. *qí-bi-ma*
4. *šu-ma* ⸢*ṭup-*⸣*pí-ki-≪na≫*
5. *mì-ma ma-num*
6. *e-zi-ba-ki-im*

Edge 7. *ig-ri*

Rev. 8. *a-na ma-ma-an*

9. *lá tù-šé-ri*
10. *a-dí a-ḫu-ki*
11. *i-lu-ku-ni-ni*
12. *ú a-na-ku*

Edge 13. *a-lá-kà-ni*
14. *ḫu-ša*!*-e*!*-ki* (or *du-na*!*-e*!*-ki*)
15. *ša-ṣé-ri*
16. *šál-ma-ku*

Translation of Pa. 43 = L 29–607

(1) Thus (says) Asshur-rabi. (3) Speak (2) to Ḫattītum, (saying): (4) If (5) anyone (6) has left (4) your tablet(s) (6) for you, (9) do not release (7) my earnings (8) to anyone.

(10) Until your brother (11) comes (12) or I (13) come, (15) cause (14) your . . . (15) to be written.

(16) I am well.

Notes on Pa. 43 = L 29–607

Line 2— Ḫattītum as a business lady married to Asshur-rabi and living in Kaniš is known from EL 141:15 (= TTC 21); BIN 6, 93:1; 182:3 (É *Ḫa-tí-tim*); 126:2 (also a letter of Asshur-rabi(?) to Ḫattītum); Gol. 18:2 (= Šil. 5 = KTK 67); and possibly TC 3, 165:17. See Larsen OACP 15 and 25 as well as B. Landsberger ArOr 18/2 (1950) 347f. for Ḫattītum's familial relations.

Line 4— The *ki-na* is written down the right edge. We have taken the *na* as a scribal error, but it is possible that the writer had another female in mind.

Line 5— *Mimma mannum*, "anyone," has the same meaning as *mì-ma-num* (= *mimma annûm*); see GKT Section 20a.

Line 10— The brother is the well-known Enlil-bāni.

Line 14— Collation verifies that the remains seem to be DU.RA.ÁŠ-*ki*. Landsberger read *ḫu-ra-áš-ki*. H. Lewy favored *tù-ra-áš-ki* but noted the possible reading *ú-tù-ra-e-ki*. Collation convinces me there is not enough space for *ú* at the beginning but that *e*! is possible. The *ra* is not at all certain, nor the *áš*. *Ḫu-ra-áš-ki* makes no sense so far as I can see, nor *tù-ra-áš-ki* or *du-ra-áš-ki*. We assume that the *ki* is "your" (feminine singular) attached to a substantive which is the direct object of the following verb.

One is tempted to read ÁŠ as *aṣ*$_{x}$ thereby forming *ḫurāṣki*, "your gold," which must be seen as problematic in two ways. First, the value *aṣ* is unattested for ÁŠ. Second, the syllabic spelling of *ḫurāṣum* is unknown to me in OA and only rarely occurs in other periods.

Another possibility is *du-na*$^{!}$*-e*$^{!}$*-ki* = "write your departure (plans)." See AHw 176b.

Still another possible reading is *ḫu-ša*$^{!}$*-e*$^{!}$*-ki* = "write down the (status of) your metal scraps." See J. Lewy OrNS 19 (1950) 18, n. 3; and B. Landsberger and K. Balkan, Belletin 14, 242, n. 40 for *ḫušā'um*.

Line 15— *Ša-ṣé-ri* is an Š imperative (feminine singular) from the root *eṣārum*, "to draw," with the possible secondary meaning "to write in the native language." The Š stem of this verb, although not indicated in CAD or AHw, is attested in ATHE 31:40 (*lu-ša-ṣé-er-ma*) and KUG 44:11 (*ša-ṣé-er-ší-na*).

Pa. 44 = L 29–610

1. 17 1/4 GÍN KÙ.[BABBAR]
2. *il*$_5$*-qí* 5 LÁ 15 ŠE GÍN [ ]
3. KÙ.BABBAR *Za-lu*$^{!}$*-li il*$_5$*-q*[*í*]
4. 1/2 MA.NA 7 GÍN 15 [ŠE KÙ.BABBAR]
5. *A-šùr-*^{d}UTU*-ši* / *il*$_5$*-*⸢*qí*⸣ [ ]
6. 4 1/2 LÁ 7 1/2 ŠE GÍN [KÙ.BABBAR]
7. [ ]-^{d}UTU *il*$_5$*-*[*qì*]

(Rest broken)

Translation of Pa. 44 = L 29–610

(1) [PN] (2) has received (1) 17 1/4 shekels of silver. (3) Zaluli has received (2) 5 shekels less 15 grains of (3) silver. (5) Asshur-shamshī has received (4) 1/2 of a mana, 7 shekels (and) 15 [grains of silver]. (7) [ ]-Shamash has received (6) 4 1/2 shekels less 7 1/2 grains [of silver]. (Rest broken)

Notes on Pa. 44 = L 29–610

This fragment begins the obverse.

Line 1— There was probably a PN in the lacuna perhaps beginning with *a*.

Line 2— The ŠE is visible after collation.

Line 3— Collation favors *Za-lu*!*-li*; the *lu* is a little damaged. This PN is unknown to me, although the similar PN *Zi-lu-lu* is well attested along with *Zi-li-li* (EL 205:2 = TC 2, 67) and the feminine PN *Zu-lu-la-a* in EL 127:9 (= CCT 1, 15b).

Line 5— Collation shows the word divider to be present after the PN and the *qí* to be mostly preserved.

Line 7— The missing first element of the PN might be one of the following: Amur-, Īdī-, Ilī, or Puzur-.

Pa. 45 = L 29–611

	1. 4 MA.NA KÙ.BABBAR
	2. *ku-nu-ki ša Šu-ma-*
	3. *li-bi*$_4$*-*⌜*lí*⌝
	4. DAM *Tár*!*-ba-li-a*!*-ili*$_5$
	5. *ni-ip-ṭur*$_4$*-ma*
	6. 4 1/2 GÍN KÙ.BABBAR
Edge	7. *im-ṭí*
Rev.	8. IGI *Da-da-a*

Translation of Pa. 45 = L 29–611

(5) We unpacked (1) (a package of) 4 manas of silver (2) (bearing) the seals (3) of Shūma-libbi-ilī (4) wife of Tarbalia-ilī (5) and (6) 4 1/2 shekels of silver (7) were missing.

(8) In the presence of Dadaja.

Notes on Pa. 45 = L 29–611

Lines 2f.— Collation reveals the last sign of the PN is a slightly damaged NI = *lí*. The PN Šūma-libbi-ilī occurs in KTH 24:28 (= EL 109); CCT 2, 24:16 (Šūma-libbi-ilia); TMH 3b:1 (= Jena 281).

Line 3 is written without the usual guide line.

Line 4— Collation shows a clear EL = *ili*$_5$ at the end of the line which for some reason was omitted from the line drawing.

The PN Tarbalia-ilī is unknown to me elsewhere. The PN *Ta-ar-ma-li-a*, taken by Garelli (AC 160) as a PN derived from a toponym, appears in TC 3, 238:A 22, B 3. It is tempting to interpret this PN in our text "(the god of) Tarmalia (is) my god." However, we must assume a scribal error since the *ba* is clear.

The two inner vertical wedges of the *tár* are very faint, but present, 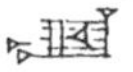 . The *a* is questionable, being very jammed.

Pa. 46 = L 29–612

1′. [ ] *iš*? [ ]
2′. [ ] 11 *ma-lá*[ ]
3′. [ ] EN *qí-bi-ma*[ ]
4′. [ ] / *a ak* [ ]
5′. [ ] *mar*? [ ]

Notes on Pa. 46 = L 29–612

No translation is possible for this small scrap beyond noting that *qí-bi-ma* in line 3′ implies that this text may have been a letter. Collation adds nothing to understanding the text.

Pa. 47 = L 29–613

1. [ ] *tí* SIG$_5$
2. [*Na-*]*ki-li-id*
3. [*Ku-*]*uk-ra-an*!
4. [ ]*aḫ-šu*
5. [ ] *li a*
6. [ ] DUMU *Ì-lí-a-lim*
7. [ ]⌈*na-*⌉*ru-uq* GIG
8. [ ] ŠE-*um*
9. [ ]*e ù* ŠE-*am*
Edge 10. [ ] *i-na*
11. [ ] *im*
Rev. 12. [ ] *dí-nu-šu-um* KÙ.BABBAR
13. [*ana*? *ša*?] *Ni-ba-a*[*s*]

14. [ ] *lu* KÙ.BABBAR ⌜*i*-⌝⌜*na*⌝
15. [*qá-qá-ad*] *šál-mì-šu-nu* [ ]
16. [*u ki-n*]*i-šu-nu ra-ki-is*
17. [IGI? x *A-šù*]*r* DUMU *Púzur-A-šùr*
18. [ ] *nim*
19. [ ] x *ni*
20. [ITI KAM *Ḫ*]*u-bu-ur*

Edge 21. [*li-*]*mu-um*

(Left Edge lost)

Notes on Pa. 47 = L 29–613

The obverse of this contract is very flat while the reverse is rounded.

Line 7— We have taken GIG as *aršātum* (see note on Pa. 38:2), although AHw 472b suggests the added possibility of *kibtum*, "wheat," for GIG.

Lines 8f.— For ŠE-*um*, see the note on Pa. 53:2 below.

Line 13— For the festival of Nibas, see Hirsch UAR 28b and 52.

Lines 14ff.— Note the formula (KÙ.BABBAR *ina qaqqad šalmišunu u kīnišunu rakis*) often (though not exclusively) used in contracts in which native Anatolians were debtors.

Line 15— Probably nothing is missing at the end of the line.

Pa. 48 = L 29–618

1′. *i-na* 2/3 M[A.NA]
2′. LÁ 1 2/3 GÍN KÙ.BAB[BAR]
3′. 2/3 ME(sic!) KÙ.KI [ ]
4′. *ša Ša-at-A-*[*šur*]
5′. 3 GÍN x [ ]
6′. 1 1/2 GÍN KÙ[ ]

Translation of Pa. 48 = L 29–618

(1′) In (or, from) 2/3 ma[na]
(2′) less 1 2/3 shekels of silv[er]

(3′) 2/3 shekel(!) of gold [ ]
(4′) of Shāt-Asshur [ ]
(5′) 3 shekels [ ]
(6′) 1 1/2 shekels of silver (or, gold) [ ]

Notes on Pa. 48 = L 29–618

Line 2′— Most of the BABBAR is present on the text.

Line 3′— According to collation the ME is clear. The remains could be  . Perhaps the scribe started to write GÍN, was distracted, and later resumed writing without finishing the GÍN.

Line 5′— The questionable sign might be *ri* according to collation.

Pa. 49 = L 29–619

1. [*ṣa-*]*ḫi-ir* GAL
2. [ ] *nàm*
3. [ ]*ma*$^{!}$ *tá-me-šu*
4. [ ] ZU.IN *Ḫa*$^{!}$*-du-e*
5. [ ]*iš-e-ma*
6. [ ]*mì*$^{!}$ *ni šu*
7. [ ] x *tí* / *a-na*
8. [ ] *Ku-lí-li*
9. [ ]*ta*$^{!}$*-aḫ-na*

Notes on Pa. 49 = L 29–619

Line 1— The *ḫi* is preserved on the text.

Line 3— Collation shows that the first sign after the lacuna is more likely to be a *ma* than *na*. *Tamešu* may be from *tamā'um*.

Line 4— Similar PNs are *Ḫa-da-a* (BIN 4, 165:10; CCT 4, 9b:20, 28; Gelb 62:3, 7, 8, 12, 24, 50; ICK 1, 96:18; 187:38; ICK 2, 81:10; 145:1, 6; TC 1, 88:1); *Ḫa-da-ḫa-da* (ICK 1, 181:36; see AC 153); *Ḫa-dí* (BIN 6, 2:2; ICK 2, 80:10; 100:x + 11; 284:x + 6; KTS 36a:2); *Ḫa-du* (BIN 4, 171: 9; KTS 51a:14); and *Ḫa-du-wa* (BIN 4, 163:2; TC 3, 158:6).

Line 8— The PN *Ku-li-li* occurs in ICK 1, 130:10. Similar PNs are *Ku-li-lá* (ICK 1, 14:14); *Ku-lí-lim* (MAH 10824:1 [Garelli RA 59 (1965) 35–37]; TC 1, 107:1; BIN 4, 23:36; 119:4; CCT 1, 19b:14; 22a:2; CCT 2, 28:9, 11; CCT 4, 29a:3, 10); and *Ku-lu-lu* (ICK 1, 21:A 1, B 19).

Pa. 50 = L 29–620

	1.	*um-ma Ḫi-na-a-ma*
	2.	*a-na A-šur-na-da*
	3.	*qí-bi-ma* 5 MA.NA
	4.	KÙ.BABBAR *i-na ša-ni-ú-tim*
	5.	*ša ni-kà-sí-*<*a*>
	6.	*ša a-na A-lá-ḫi*$^{!}$*-im*
	7.	*i-pu-lu-ni*
Edge	8.	5 MA.NA KÙ.BABBAR
Rev.	9.	*i-a-tí* / *i-lá-kam*
	10.	*tí-ir-tí* / *A-lá-ḫi-im*
	11.	*E-lá-ma* / *ub-lam*
	12.	*um-ma šu-ut-ma*
	13.	*a-ṣé-er* / *A-mur-Išt*[*ar*]
	14.	*ú A-šur-na-da*[ ]
	15.	*li-ìš-pu-ur-ma*
	16.	*i-na* KÙ.BABBAR-*pì-a*
	17.	*li-dí-nu-šum*
Edge	18.	*i-na* KÙ.BABBAR-*pì-šu*$^{!}$
	19.	5 MA.NA
Left Edge	20.	*li-qí-ma* / *tí-ir-ta-kà*
	21.	*li-li-kam*

Translation of Pa. 50 = L 29–620

(1) Thus (says) Ḫinnā. (3) Speak (2) to Asshur-nādā, (saying): (8) 5 manas of silver (4) from others (9) will come to me— (3) (that is,) the 5 manas (4) of silver (5) belonging to my account (6) which (7) they have paid back (6) to Al(i)-aḫum.

(11) Elamma has brought me (10) Al(i)-aḫum's report. (12) Thus he (said): (15) Let him write (13) to Amur-Ishtar (14) and Asshur-nādā, (15) and (17) let them give to him (16) some of my silver.

(18) From his silver (20) take (19) 5 manas (20) and (21) let (20) your report (21) come to me.

Notes on Pa. 50 = L 29–620

Line 1— See AOATT 319 and OACP 57 for Ḫinnā.

Line 6— The PN *A-lá-ḫi*[!]*-im* is not perfectly clear due to faulty writing of the *ḫi*; *bi* is also possible but with a Winkelhaken missing. We prefer *ḫi*, since *A-lá-ḫi-im* appears in line 10 with the *ḫi* clear.

Line 18— Collation shows that the *šu* is very small and could be *ma*, but we prefer *šu* on the basis of context.

Pa. 51 = L 29–622

1. 50 MA.NA KÙ.BABBAR
2. *ku-nu-ki ša A-lá-ḫi-im*
3. *a-na A-šur-ṣú-lu-li*
4. *áp-qí-id*
5. IGI *A-šur-i-dí*
6. DUMU *A-šur-ma-lik*
7. IGI *I-ku-pí-a*

Rev. 8. DUMU *E-dí-na-a*

9. IGI *Ú-zu-a* DUMU
10. *A-bi*$_4$*-li-a*

Translation of Pa. 51 = L 29–622

(4) I entrusted (1) 50 manas of silver (2) (bearing) the seals of Al(i)-aḫum (3) to Asshur-ṣulūlī.

(5) In the presence of Asshur-īdī (6) son of Asshur-malik, (7) in the presence of Ikū(n)-pīa (8) son of Edinā, (9) in the presence of Uzu'a son of (10) Abī-(i)lia.

Notes on Pa. 51 = L 29–622

Line 8— Mrs. Lewy suggested the PN might be read *Šu-A-na*, but later collation verifies that *E-dí-na-a* is correct.

Line 10— This spelling of the PN occurs in BIN 6, 91:6. Similar PNs are: *A-bi$_4$-li* (TMH 28d:x + 3 = Jena 300); *A-bi-ili$_5$* (TMH 6d:b, x + 8 = Jena 394); *A-bi-ì-lí* (KUG 10:A 6, B 8); *A-bi$_4$-ì-lí-[šu]* (TC 3, 191: 45); *A-bi$_4$-lá* (TC 2, 1:35; 47:19; and Chantre 4:13 [*A-bi-la*] *et passim*); *A-bi$_4$-i-lá* (CCT 4, 23a:6); *A-bi$_4$-ì-lí* (TC 3, 129:y + 2); *A-bu-um*-DINGIR (CCT 6, 47a:7); and *A-bu*-DINGIR (KTH 13:5, 46).

Pa. 52 = L 29–623

	1. 1 *ṭup-pá-am na-áš-pár-tám*
	2. *ša ku-nu-ki-a ša a-wa-tum*
	3. *ša Šu-Ištar* DUMU DINGIR-*iš-tí-kál*
	4. *gam-ra-ni a-na* DU$_{10}$-*ṣí-lá-A-šur*
	5. *ap-qí-id šu-ma ma-lá*
	6. *a-wa-tum gam-ra-ni*
Edge	7. KÙ.BABBAR *a-ša ki-ma*
	8. *i-a-tí lá iš-ta-qal*
Rev.	9. *tí-ir-tí ša-zu-úz-tí-a*
	10. *i-lá-kam-ma*
	11. *na-áš-pár-tám ša ku-nu-ki-a*
	12. DU$_{10}$-*ṣí-lá-A-šur ú-ša-ra-ma*
	13. *ṭup-pu-a ṭup-pu-ú-a-ma*
	14. IGI *Li-ip-ta-nim*
Edge	15. DUMU *Lá-li-im*
	16. IGI *Ḫa-nu-nu* DUB.SAR

Translation of Pa. 52 = L 29–623

(5) I entrusted (2) to Ṭāb-ṣilla-Asshur (1) one message tablet (2) (bearing) my seals concerning the matters (4) which had been settled (3) involving Shū-Ishtar son of Ilish-tikal. (5) If, in accordance with (6) the matters that have been settled, (7) the silver (8) has not been weighed out (7) to (8) my (7) representative, (9) the report of my agent (10) will come to me, and (12) Ṭāb-ṣilla-Asshur will release for me (11) the message (bearing) my seals, (12) and (13) (then) my tablets (will truly be) my tablets!

(14) In the presence of Lip(i)t-Anum (15) son of Lalum, (16) in the presence of Ḫanunu the scribe.

Notes on Pa. 52 = L 29–623

Lines 1 and 11— Note that the *ṭuppam našpartam* of line 1 is called simply *našpartam* in line 11.

Lines 2–4— This clause, as well as that in lines 5f., may be interpreted in two ways: 1) *ša a-wa-tum . . . gamrāni*, "that the matters are (being) settled," or 2) 1 *ṭuppam našpartam . . . ša a-wa-tim ša* PN *gamrāni*, "we are settling the (matter of) one message tablet of the affairs of PN." We favor the first interpretation because of the rarity of TUM = *tim*. See also BIN 6, 201:24f., where *a-wa-tù-šu-nu iš-tí* PN *gam-ra-ni* roughly parallels our case.

Line 14— Lip(i)t-Anum son of Lalum is known from CCT 1, 4:3f. (= EL 225) and KUG 51:10. Lip(i)t-Anum without patronym occurs in BIN 4, 125:2; Gelb 56:38 (*ḫamuštum*); 59:33 (*ḫamuštum*); EL 226:39 (= VAT 13513, *ḫamuštum*); and 263:30 (= Tübingen 1).

Line 15— For Lalum father of Lip(i)t-Anum, see note on line 14. Lalum alone appears rather frequently. É *Lalim* occurs in VAT 13458:25 (EL II p. 103, n. a on p. 104) and Schaeffer 22:20 (Garelli RA 58 [1964] 124–128). The *ḫamuštum*-period of Lulum and Aninum occurs in Rouen 3:13f. (= HG 72 in Garelli RA 51 [1957] 9f.).

Line 16— Ḫanunu the scribe (DUB.SAR) is known from VAT 13539:y + 4 (= EL 111); VAT 13505:x + 11 (unpublished, but mentioned by Lewy EL I p. 98, n. b); and TC 1, 81:33.

Pa. 53 = L 29–624

1. 3 *na-ru-uq*
2. ŠE-*am Šu-Be-lim*
3. *me-ra-šu*
4. *i-li-kam-ma*

Edge 5. *a-na Ku-lu-ma-a*

Rev. 6. *a-dí-in*

Translation of Pa. 53 = L 29–624

(3) His son (4) came (with) (1) 3 sacks of (2) wheat of Shū-Bēlum's, (4) and (6) I gave (them) (5) to Kulumā.

Notes on Pa. 53 = L 29–624

Line 2— Kennedy and Garelli (JCS 4 [1960] 19) followed H. Lewy (JAOS 76 [1956] 201–204) who argued that *aršātum* was barley while *še'um* was wheat. CAD A_2 309 took *še'um* to mean barley and *aršātum*, wheat or some form of barley. Mrs. Lewy showed that *še'um* was more expensive than *aršātum*, which led her to her conclusion. One might argue that *še'um* designated better quality barley and *aršātum* ("dirty"), a lower-grade barley. But this suggestion leaves unanswered the question of what word designated wheat in OA since, as Mrs. Lewy showed, GIG and *uṭṭutum* sold at the same price as *aršātum*, while *kibtum* does not appear written syllabically in OA. We, therefore, follow Mrs. Lewy's explanation.

Line 3— *Me-ra-šu* is singular nominative plus *šu* ("his") as in EL 202:8 (= Gol. 24 = Šil. 6 = KTK 101) and EL 8:2 (= TCL 1, 240). See GAG Paradigm 4 (p. 6*) and Gelb p. 22.

Pa. 54 = L 29–625

1. 6 *na-ru-uq*
2. *qé-ma-am*
3. *a-na be-el* É*-tim*
4. *ša mu-ṣí-im*
5. *ni-im-du-ud*

Translation of Pa. 54 = L 29–625

(5) We measured out (1) 6 sacks of (2) meal (3) to the chief of the (4) customs'(?) (3) house.

Notes on Pa. 54 = L 29–625

Line 4— Veenhof (AOATT 231, n. 362) is unsure of the relation between *mūṣi'um* and *waṣītum*, but assumes with Garelli (regarding MAH 16209:19 [RA 59 (1965) 156–160]) and Hecker (GKT Section 97e) that *mūṣi'um* is a person, while noting that von Soden (AHw 679a) understands the term as "departure tax." Veenhof's citing of CAD A_1 335a is a wrong reference.

The wording of our text does not favor either interpretation of *mūṣi'um*. *Ša mūṣîm* may be in apposition to *bēl bītim*: "we measured out . . . to the owner or chief of the house, who (is also) the comptroller." The wording would also allow us to translate the phrase: "to the chief of the house of comptrollers," since, as Garelli shows (RA 59 [1965] 160), *mūṣi'um* may be considered a collective in MAH 16209. *Bīt mūṣîm* occurs in TC 3, 161:5 and *bīt rabi mūṣê* in CCT 1, 38c:6. Garelli (AC 217) took *rabi mūṣê* to mean "chief of tradesmen." See also J. Lewy KTH p. 15. We must leave this question open for now.

The reverse of this tablet is not inscribed.

Pa. 55 = L 29–628

Obv. 1. *um-ma* [ ]*ri*$^{!}$*-iš-ma*
2. *a-na* [*A-š*]*ur-i-dí*
3. 1 MA.NA 6$^{?}$ GÍN [ ]
4. ⸢x⸣ [ ]
(rest of Obverse destroyed)
Rev. 1′. [ ]⸢x⸣ *a-*⸢*ma*$^{?}$⸣ [ ]
2′. [ ]*-at* KÙ.BABBAR [ ]
3′. [ ]⸢x⸣ *lu im* [ ]
4′. [ ] *iš-tí* [ ]
5′. [ ]*ku*$^{?}$ *a-ḫu* [x]
6′. [*i-*]*ša-me-ma* x[ ]
7′. [ ]*i ta*$^{!}$ *ni-a-tí*[ ]
8′. [ ] *iš-tí a* ⸢x⸣ *lá*$^{?}$ *me*[ ]
9′. [*n*]*a-pá-áš-ta-kà ma*$^{?}$ ⸢x⸣[ ]
10′. [ ] KÙ.BABBAR *ma-a-ad* ⸢x⸣ [ ]
11′. [ ] x x / *at* ⸢x⸣ [ ]
12′. [ ]⸢x⸣ *ba* [ ] / *lá ḫu um*
(Left Edge lost)

Notes on Pa. 55 = L 29–628

Line 1— One or two signs are missing in the lacuna.

I know of only one OA PN ending in *ri-iš*, namely, DINGIR-*e-ri-iš* in BIN 4, 32:5 (DINGIR-*e-ri-šu* in line 15).

Other PNs ending in *iš* are: *Ḫu-zi-iš* (BIN 6, 145:11), *Ku-zu-bi-iš*$^{?}$ (ICK 2, 99:15), *Ta-ak-ni-iš* (ATHE 5:A 18, B 2; KTS 33a:4; TC 1,

90a:3; 90b:3), *Ta-li-iš* (ATHE 6:A 4, B 2, 7), *Tù-uḫ-ni-iš* (ATHE 67:16$^{?}$; BIN 4, 113:1, 8, 12; CCT 6, 16b:35), and *Wa-al-ḫi-iš* (ICK 1, 190:25; see AC 148).

Line 2— The *šur* is partially preserved.

Line 3— The numeral is either 6 or 8.

Line 7′— *Ta* is more likely than *ša*.

Line 9′— The sign following *napaštaka* is more like *ma* or *ku* than the line drawing suggests.

Line 10′— Before the lacuna 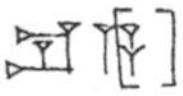 may be left or perhaps 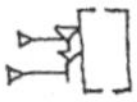 .

Line 11′— What Mrs. Lewy drew looks like [ ] *ṭup-pu* [x] *šál* x [ ]. The signs are not this plain on the tablet. The remains may be interpreted as [ ] *ra*$^{?}$*-bi*$^{?}$ / *at* [ ] or as [ ] GA *tim* / *at* [ ].

Line 12′— The last signs may be the PN ⌜*A*-⌝*lá-ḫu-um*.

Pa. 56 = L 29–629

1′. [*La*$^{!}$-]*qí-ip* [ ]
2′. [*š*]*a*$^{?}$ / 1/2 MA.NA [ ]
3′. [*š*]*a*$^{?}$ *Lá-qí-ip* [ ]
1″. [*t*]*a*$^{?}$ [ ]
2″. [ ] *ku* x *šu*$^{?}$ *da*$^{!}$ [ ]
3″. [*ṭ*]*up-pu-šu ša* 1 5/6 MA.⌜NA⌝[ ]
4″. [*ṭup-*]*pu-šu* / *ša* 1/3 MA.NA KÙ.BABBAR
5″. [ ] *ni tí* [ ]

Notes on Pa. 56 = L 29–629

It is impossible to judge which is the Obverse and which is the Reverse.

Line 1′— Collation favors *ip* over Mrs. Lewy's ZU.

Line 2″ remains unclear after collation. The *šu* may be a partially destroyed *na*.

Line 3″— Collation verifies 5/6 rather than 2/3.

Line 5″— Collation shows this partial line omitted by Mrs. Lewy.

Pa. 57 = L 29–631

1. 1 1/3 MA.NA 22 1/2 ŠE
2. KÙ.BABBAR *ṣa-ru-pá-am*
3. *i-li-bi*
4. *Šu-ma-li-bi*$_4$*-A-šur*
5. *A-ḫu-wa-qar*
6. *i-šu*
7. IGI *A-mur*-DINGIR!
8. IGI *En-um-A-šur*
9. DUMU *A-šur-i-mì-*⸢*tí*⸣

Translation of Pa. 57 = L 29–631

(5) Aḫu-waqar (6) has (a debt of) (1) 1 1/3 manas (and) 22 1/2 grains of (2) refined silver (3) against the account of (4) Shumma-libbi-Asshur.

(7) In the presence of Amur-ilī, (8) in the presence of Ennum-Asshur (9) son of Asshur-imittī.

Notes on Pa. 57 = L 29–631

Line 1— The second ŠE is not on the tablet.
Line 3— Note *ina libbi* for the usual *ana ṣēr*.
Line 4— On the PN Šumma-libbi-DN, see CAD L 171a.
Line 7— The DINGIR is poorly preserved on the tablet.

Pa. 58 = UM 41–41–2

1. *a-na Bi-tí-tí* / *Ma-ṣí-ì-lí*
2. *A-lá-ḫi-im A-šùr*-GAL *Aḫ-Ša-lim*
3. *I-ku-pí-a* [[x x]]
4. *ù Šé-ṣur*!*-Da-gán*
5. *qí-bi*$_4$*-ma um-ma Zu-ri-i-ma*
6. *a-na Šé-ṣur*!*-Da-gán qí-bi*$_4$*-ma*
7. 1/3 MA.NA KÙ.BABBAR *a-ta* / *ú a-bu-kà*

8. *iš-tù li-mì-im I-dí-a-*⸢*bi*$_4$*-*⸣*im*
9. *ḫa-bu-lá-tù-nu* 1 GÍN TA *ṣí-ib-tám*
10. *i-*ITI 1 KAM *tù-ṣa-ba a-ḫa-ma*
11. 1/3 MA.NA KÙ.BABBAR *a-na I-*⸢*li-*⸣*ib-li-bi*$_4$
12. *ḫa-bu-*≪*bu-*≫*lá-tù-nu-ma*
13. *tap-nu-a-nim-ma* KÙ.BABBAR *a-na*
14. *I-li-ib-li-bi áš-qúl-ma*
15. *i-na e-ṣí-im* / *ú-šé-li-ku-nu*

Edge 16. *ù* KÙ.BABBAR *ša iš-tù*
17. *li-mì-im Ì-lí-a-lim*

Rev. 18. 1 GÍN TA*-ma* / *tù-ṣa-ba*
19. *a-bu-kà* / *Ar-mì-li* KÙ.BABBAR
20. *ú ṣí-ba-sú* / *mì-iš-li-šu*
21. *ú-ša-bi*$_4$*-a-ni-ma ṭup-pá-am*
22. *ša ku-nu-ki-a* / *a-dí-šu-um ša a-na*
23. *mì-iš-li-šu* / *lá a-du-ru-šu-ni*
24. *a-na mì-iš-al* KÙ.BABBAR *ú ṣí-ib-tim*
25. *a-ta* / *ta-za-za-ni* / *ṭup-pu-um*
26. *šu-ut ša ku-nu-ki* / É *Bu-ra-a i-ba-ší*
27. *a-na Bi*$_4$*-tí-tí* / *ú ša ki-ma*
28. *i-a-tí qí-bi*$_4$*-ma* 1/3 MA.NA KÙ.BABBAR
29. *mì-iš-lu-šu a-na* 3 1/2 MA.NA KÙ.BABBAR
30. *i-tù-ar-šu* / KÙ.BABBAR *ú ṣí-ba-sú*
31. [*a*!*-ṣ*]*é-er ṭup-pè-e-šu* / *li-ik-nu-uk*!*-ma*
32. [ ]*ṭup-pè-e-šu a-na ša ki-ma*
33. *šu-a-tí* / *lá-dí-in* / *a-na Bi*$_4$*-tí-tí*
34. *qí-bi*$_4$*-ma* / *a-dí* / *iš-ri-šu*

Edge 35. *áš-pu-ra-kum* / *u*$_4$*-ma-kál*
36. *i-zi-iz-ma* / É*-bi*$_4$*-sú*

Left Edge 37. *ú*! [*ma-la*] *i-šu-ú* / *a-na* KÙ.BABBAR*-pì*!
38. *dí-i*[*n-m*]*a* ⸢*Ma-ṣí-*⸣*ì-lí ú I-ku-pì-a*
39. [*iš-tí A-šur-*]GAL! KÙ.BABBAR *lu-ub-lu-nim-ma*
40. *ṭup-pè-e-šu* <*a-da-an*>

Translation of Pa. 58 = UM 41–41–2

(5) Speak (1) to Bititi, Maṣṣi-ilī, (2) Al(i)-aḫum, Asshur-rabi, (3) Ikū(n)-pīa, (4) and Shēṣur-Dagan. (5) Thus (says) Zurī. (6) Speak to Shēṣur-Dagan, (saying): (7) You and your father (9) owe (7) 1/3 of a

mana of silver (8) (counting) from the eponymy of Īdī-abum. (10) You must pay (9) one shekel (10) per month (9) per (mana) as interest. (10) Besides (12) you owe (11) 1/3 of a mana of silver to Iliblibi, (12) but you appealed to me and (14) I weighed out (13) the silver to (14) Iliblibi, and (so) (15) recently I have summoned you (into court). (16) So (18) you must add (as interest) (16) the silver which is (dated) from (17) the eponymy of Ilī-ālum (18) at the rate of one shekel per (mana per month). Your father Armili (21) has paid (20) half (19) the silver and its interest (21) and (22) I have given to him (21) a tablet (22) (bearing) my seals. (22) In respect to (23) the (other) half of it (22) about which (23) I did not bother him, (25) you must stand good for me (24) for half of the silver and the interest. (26) That (25) tablet (26) (bearing) the seals of the house of Burā exists.

(28) Speak (27) to Bititi and (28) my (27) representative, (saying), (29) Half of the (28) 1/3 of a mana of silver (20) will return (29) for the 3 1/2 manas of silver, (and) (31) let him seal (20) the silver and its interest payment (31) on his tablets and (33) let me give (32) his tablets to (33) his representative.

(34) Speak (33) to Bititi, (saying): (35) I have written to you (34) ten times! (36) He has waited (stood) long enough (a while)! So (and) (38) sell (36) his house (37) or [whatever] he has for silver (38) and(!) (39) let (38) Maṣṣi-ilī and Ikū(n)-pīa (39) bring the silver here [with Asshur-rabi], and (40) his tablets <I will give.>

Notes on Pa. 58 = UM 41–41–2

Lines 1, 27, and 33— The PN Bititi is unattested elsewhere so far as I know.

Line 3— Following the PN there are probably two erased signs.

Lines 4 and 6— The PN *Šé-ṣur*[!]*-Da-gán* is not known from elsewhere although *Šé-ṣú-ur* is found in KTH 5:16; BIN 6, 226:4, case 3 and 9. The *ṣur* in both cases is drawn more like *ul*, 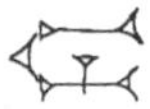 ; but *Ší-ul-Da-gán* makes no sense.

Line 5— The PN *Zu-ri-i* occurs in BIN 6, 68:3.

Lines 11 and 14— The PN *I-li-ib-li-bi* occurs nowhere else.

Line 13— The tablet clearly has *tap-nu-a-nim-ma* from *panā'um*, "to turn to." J. Lewy OrNS 15 (1946) 385, n. 2, in discussing TC 1, 51:3–11, suggested the secondary meaning "to appeal to," which fits our context admirably. See also AHw 822b.

Line 15— *Ina (w)ēṣim* = "in a little, shortly, soon." See GKT Sections 26a, 96d, and 40d (*ēṣiš*). "Recently" fits our circumstances considering the tense of the verb.

Line 19— The PN *Ar-mì-li* is unknown to me elsewhere. It seems to fit that type of PN ending in *il* or *ili*; see Garelli AC 152f.

Line 23— There are two roots *adārum* conjugated alike (*īdur, iddar, adir*). Our context favors "to be worried, disturbed, restless" (CAD A_1 103ff.).

Lines 24f.— *Ana . . . tazzazanni*, "you will stand for . . . ," means "take the responsibility for."

Collation verifies that the scribe wrote *mì-iš-al* for the expected *mì-ša-al*.

Line 26— The PN *Bu-ra-a* or *Pu-ra-a* is unattested. *Bu-ra-Ma-ma* occurs in EL 221:6 (= TC 1, 64). The PN may be a hypocoristicon ending in *-a* from *būrum*, "offspring"; see Garelli AC 128–130.

Line 30— Collation shows a word divider between *itu'aršu* and KÙ.BABBAR.

The *šu* of *itu'aršu* is problematic since the G of *tu'ārum* is intransitive. Perhaps we have a scribal error for *šum* or the *šu* should be omitted altogether.

Veenhof (AOATT 351 and 365) remarks on the idiom *luqūtum ana* KÙ.BABBAR *ituwar*.

Line 31— We restore *a* in the lacuna; there is not enough space for *i*. The *uk* of *liknukma* is squeezed on the right edge.

Line 32— Probably nothing is missing although there is room for one sign in the lacuna.

Line 34— For *adi išrīšu*, see GKT Sections 71a and b.

Line 35— For *ūmakkal*, "a while," see GKT Sections 65a and 102i, but "a (whole) day" in GAG Sections 62h and 72b.

Lines 37–40 are hard to read since they are tightly written on the left edge.

Line 37— Following the partially preserved *ú* there remain traces of possibly two signs, but the area is so smudged that they are completely illegible. We have restored *mala* to satisfy *i-šu-ú* which seems to be a subjunctive. The word divider is verified by collation.

The *pì* of KÙ.BABBAR-*pì* is possible but not certain.

Line 39— The front part of the line is badly smudged and is anybody's guess. The GAL is less damaged but not sure. The PN Asshur-rabi is suggested from the fact that he is mentioned in line 2 as an addressee. The end of the line is not as well preserved as Mrs. Lewy's drawing would suggest.

Line 40— The word *ṭup-pè-e-šu* is tightly squeezed in the center bottom of the left edge where the text is a little thicker. The *ṭup* is less well preserved than Mrs. Lewy's drawing shows. Nothing is missing before *ṭuppēšu*.

The scribe obviously ran out of space to complete the message as seen from the *ma* enclitic on the verb in line 39. We have supplied what must have been in Zurī's mind to say as suggested from lines 32f. As soon as he receives the silver, he will have receipt-tablets drawn up for Šēṣur-Dagan.

Pa. 59 = CBS 4057

1′. [ ] GAL *na* x *iš*? [ ]
2′. [ ] *tim*
3′. [ ] *ma*? *a-na*
4′. [ ] ILLAT-*tám*
5′. [ ] *ma ḫu-lu-qá-ú*
6′. [ ] *ú-ni-ma*
7′. [*a-*]*šar*

Notes on Pa. 59 = CBS 4057

The preserved portion of this text is the right-hand middle of one side.

Line 5′— The term *ḫuluqqā'um* alternates with *ḫaluqqā'um*. See GKT Section 9a.

Pa. 60 = CBS 4072

Obv. 1′. [ ] *na*? [ ]
2′. [ ] x *a* [ ]
3′. [ ] *na a m*[*a*?]
4′. [ ] x *id*? [ ]
5′. [ ] *bu a*? [ ]
Rev. 1″. [*A*?*-šur*?*-*]*na-da* [ ]
2″. [ ] *A-šùr* [ ]
3″. [ ] *nim* [ ]

Note on Pa. 60 = CBS 4072

This scrap is the middle right portion of what may have been a witnessed document since the remains of lines 1″–3″ suggest a list of witnesses.

Pa. 61 = CBS 5675

Obv.	1′. [	] x *ta* [ ]
	2′. [	] *na-áš-a-ku-*[*um*?]
	3′. [	*m*]*a*? *i a bi sú* [ ]
	4′. [	] 10 GÍN *šé-bi*$_4$*-la*[*m*]
	5′. [	] *ší*?*-i-be* [ ]
Rev.	1″. [	] *áš*? *ra* [ ]
	2″. [	*l*]*i*? *ša lim* [ ]
	3″. [	] *tí-ir-ta-kà* [ ]
	4″. [	] *li-li-k*[*am*?]
	5″. [	Ḫ]I?.A *ku*[ ]

Notes on Pa. 61 = CBS 5675

The remains are the weathered left part of a tablet.

Line 1′— H. and J. Lewy's collation notes read this line: 4 *ku-ta-ni*[ ]. However, the remains are not clear.

Line 3′— J. Lewy read: *ṣubātum i-a-am ku*?[ ]. The remains are more like H. Lewy's drawing, however.

Line 2″— The remains may favor [ ] *ta-ša-me* [ ].

Pa. 62 = CBS 4074

Obv.	1′.	*qí-bi-ma um-*[*ma*]
	2′.	*i-na Kà-ni-i*[*š*]
	3′.	*šál-ma-ku i-*[*na*]
	4′.	*pá-aq-da-*[*ni*?]
Left Edge	1″.	[ ] DUMU *la* [ ]
	2″.	[ ] *tí a li* [ ]
	3″.	[ ] x *ma šé* [ ]

Notes on Pa. 62 = CBS 4074

What remains legible is the left upper part of a letter written in a beautiful hand.

Line 1″— What we have read as *la* may be *at*, hence forming *mērat*.

Line 2″— J. Lewy suggested *a-li-*[*ki-im*].

Line 3″— J. Lewy proposed *šé-b*[*i_4-lam*$^{?}$].

Collation verifies that the three partial lines labeled "Rev." in Mrs. Lewy's drawing are not a part of CBS 4074. Their origin is unknown to me.

Pa. 63 = CBS 4054

One Side 1′. [ ] GÍN KÙ.GI [ ]

2′. *lá* ⸢*ba*⸣ *šu kam* [ ]

3′. *ša a-mu-tim* [ ]

4′. *du-dí-*⸢*na-*⸣*tim* [ ]

5′. *du*$^{!}$*-dí-*⸢*na-*⸣*tu* [ ]

6′. *ša a* x x [ ]

7′. *na-aḫ-lá-*<*áp-*>⸢*tu*⸣ [ ]

Other Side 1″. 4 *na-*⸢*ru-*⸣*qá*$^{!}$*-*[*tim*$^{?}$]

2″. ⸢*ša*⸣ *ú-nu-t*[*im*]

3″. *8 ta*$^{!}$*-*<*ma-*>*lá-*[*gi_5*$^{?}$]

4″. *ta-ma-lá* [ ]

5″. *i* x *ni* [ ]

6″. *i-pá-ni-*[*im*$^{?}$]

Notes on Pa. 63 = CBS 4054

It is impossible to be sure which side is obverse and which is reverse. Each side starts and finishes without exhausting the available space. The inscription of the whole text is less than sharp and very hard to read. Mrs. Lewy's collation notes state: "surface is almost flat, as if polished to erase the scripts."

Line 6′— J. Lewy thought this line should read *ša a-mu-tim* [ ].

Line 7′— *Naḫlaptum* is translated "cloak" in AOATT 150 and 178, but "garment, mantle" in AHw 715a.

Lines 3″ff.— For *tamalagum*, see the note on Pa. 37:5. J. Lewy suggested that line 4″ should read: *ta-ma-lá-*[*ga-am*].

Pa. 64 = CBS 11092

Obv. 1′. [ ] x *a* x [ ]
2′. [ ]*kà-*$il_5^{!}$*-šu* x [ ]
3′. [ ] *a na* (or *šur*) x [ ]
4′. [ ] 1 GIŠ GA [ ]
5′. [ ] x [ ]
6′. [ ] *ta-áš-ku* x [ ]
7′. [ ] x *a na* (or *šur*) [ ]
8′. [ ] x KI *šum* [ ]
9′. [ ] *ir* (or *ni*) x x [ ]
Rev. 1″. [ ] *a* x [ ]
2″. [ ] *a-dí-na-k*[*um*$^{?}$]
3″. [ ] *na ku*$^{?}$ *ma* [ ]
4″. [ ] *ak*$^{?}$ *lá* [ ]
5″. [ ] *lá* [ ]

Notes on Pa. 64 = CBS 11092

When collating this text I discovered that what Mrs. Lewy drew in HUCA 39/40 (1969/70) 82 for line 2′ is not certain. I also found the four additional fragmentary lines following line 5′ proceeding without break to the five fragmentary lines on the other side.

Line 4′ might be reconstructed 1 GIŠ.GA.ZUM = *mušṭum*, "comb." See AHw 687a and AOATT 107, n. 180.

Pa. 65 = CBS 11095

1′. [ ] AN
2′. [ ] *aḫ šu*
3′. [ ] *ša*
4′. [*m*]*a*$^{?}$*-an*
5′. [ ] *ta-kà*
6′. [ ] *at*
1″. [ ] AN

2″. [*A*-]*šur*-GAL
3″. [ ] *u*$_4$-*me-e*
4″. [ ] AN
Edge 5″. [TÚG$^?$]*bu*-⌜*ra*-⌝*um*

Note on Pa. 65 = CBS 11095

Line 5″— *Bu-ra-um* is variously understood. AHw 142a translates "reed mat, carpet," while CAD B 328b suggests some kind of garment whose name is derived from a GN. Veenhof (AOATT 173f.) argues that *burā'um* designated an expensive garment of Mesopotamian origin.

Pa. 66 = CBS 11091

1′. [ ] *ra* (or *ak*) [ ]
2′. [ ] DU GA [ ]
3′. [ ] *lá* [ ]

Pa. 67 = CBS 11093

1′. [ ] DU *um* [ ]
2′. [ ] *ki-in* [ ]
3′. [ ] *a ki bi* x [ ]
4′. [ ] x *lá aḫ ma* [ ]
5′. [ ] ⌜*a*⌝ (or ⌜ZA⌝) [ ]

Note on Pa. 67 = CBS 11093

Line 2′ perhaps may be restored to give the PN [*Pu-šu-*]*ki-in*. Otherwise nothing may be read.

Pa. 68 = CBS 5669

1′. [ ] x
2′. [ ] 5$^?$ MA.⌜NA⌝

3′. [ ] lu DU [ ]
4′. [ ] ḫa-ma 2 1/2$^{?}$ GÍN [ ]
5′. [ ] bu GI$^{!}$ IGI A-šur[ ]
6′. [ ]⌈i-ba-⌉ri-a x [ ]
7′. [ ] a x x [ ]
Edge 1″. [ ] x x [ ]
2″. [ ] da šu [ ]
3″. [ ] x x [ ]
4″. [ ]
5″. [ ] x ma x [ ]
6″. [ ] ba a [ ]
7″. [ ] ša i-na ṭup[ ]
8″. [ ] ú-lá aḫ-dá-ku-nu-[tí]
9″. [ ] DU ma ší-i[m]
Edge 10″. [ ] ší ni x [ ]

Note on Pa. 68 = CBS 5669

The surface of this text is badly eroded. In line 5′ we obviously have a PN beginning with Asshur. Line 8″ seems to have the statement "I was not happy with you." See CAD Ḫ 25ff.

Pa. 69 = CBS 5672

1′. [ ] ni a [ ]
2′. [ ] a i [ ]
3′. [ ] x bi ma [ ]
4′. [ ] ba a [ ]
5′. [ ] ma [ ]

Note on Pa. 69 = CBS 5672

Pa. 69 is a small fragment from near the middle of the text preserving a few signs near the end of the lines. Not one complete word is preserved.

Pa. 70 = CBS 5677

Obv.	1′.	*a-na A-šur-*[ ]
	2′.	*qí*[ ]
	3′.	[ ]
	4′.	[ ]
	5′.	[ ]
	6′.	[ ]
Rev.	1″.	[ ]
	2″.	x *ku* [ ] *iš* x [ ]
	3″.	x *lá-*[*dí*?-]*in* [ ]
	4″.	*me* [ ] *zi-ib* [ ]
	5″.	x *ma* [ ] *ma* [ ]

Note on Pa. 70 = CBS 5677

The surface of Pa. 70 is badly weathered. The beginning of a PN is visible in line 1′ beginning with Asshur. We may restore line 2′ *qí-*[*bi-ma*].

Pa. 71 = CBS 5674

Edge	1′.	[ ] *šál a* [ ]
	2′.	[ ] ⌜GA⌝
Rev.	3′.	[ ] x
	4′.	[ ] ⌜*ul*⌝ x
	5′.	[ ] *li* x
	6′.	[ ] *ba me-tù-ni*
	7′.	[ ] *ba* ZU-*ú-ni*
	8′.	[ ] KÙ.BABBAR *ša* [ ]
	9′.	[ ] KÙ.BABBAR x [ ]
	10′.	[ ] x *im-tim* KÙ.BABBAR [ ]

Notes on Pa. 71 = CBS 5674

Pa. 71 is the upper right corner of a tablet written in small script. Hardly anything remains except KÙ.BABBAR in lines 8′, 9′, and 10′. We may have [*ší-*]*im-tim*, "stipulated amount," in line 10′.

Pa. 72 = CBS 5679

Obv.	1′. *lu* [ ]
	2′. *lá* x [ ]
	3′. 1 1/2 M[A.NA]
	4′. *a*-⌜*na*⌝ [ ]
Edge	5′. *a* [ ]
Rev.	6′. 1/2 MA.[NA]
	7′. *mu*-TA[ ]
	8′. *i li* [ ]
	9′. 3 1/3 ⌜GÍN⌝[ ]

Notes on Pa. 72 = CBS 5679

Line 7′ may be read *mu-ṭa-*[*e*], "deficiency." See AOATT 47–53. Line 8′ may be *illi*[*bbi*] = *ina libbi*.

Pa. 73 = CBS 5670

1′. [ ] x *ra* [ ]
2′. [ ] *sú ri ni* [ ]
3′. [ ] *zu-ta-a* [ ]
4′. [ ] ZU *ni* 10 u_4-[*me*?]
5′. [ ]⌜KI⌝ *šu-ma* / *Šu*-⌜*Ištar*⌝[ ]
6′. [*n*]*a-ku ša* É x [ ]
7′. [ ] x *a-wi-lu* [ ]
8′. [ ] x *im ša* [ ]
9′. [ ] *ma-ni-i*[*m*]
10′. [ ] ID [ ]

Notes on Pa. 73 = CBS 5670

Pa. 73 is a fragment from the middle of one side of a document, perhaps a letter.

Line 2′ may contain either the particle *issurri*, "certainly," or *assurri*, "in any case." See GKT Section 106b.

We may restore the PNs [*Bu-*]*zu-ta-a* in line 3′ and *Šu-Ištar* in line 5′.

Pa. 74 = CBS 4073

1′. [ ] *ša* [ ]
2′. [ ]-*qí-id ú* [ ]
3′. [AN]ŠE^{ḫi}-*kà* SÍG [ ]
4′. [ ] x *iš-tí* [ ]
5′. [ ] x *ur-da-ni* [ ]
6′. [ ] 4 (or 2) GÍN KÙ.⌜BABBAR⌝ [ ]

Notes on Pa. 74 = CBS 4073

Pa. 74 is a weathered small fragment, probably from the middle of the obverse. It is irregularly broken.

Line 2′ may be *apqid* or *ipqid*.

The questionable sign in line 4′ before *iš-tí* may be *lu*, *ku*, or the latter part of SIPA perhaps in the PN [*A-šur*-S]IPA or [^{d}IM-S]IPA.

The sign beginning line 5′ was probably *ṭù* to form the well attested imperative *ṭurdanni*, "send, dispatch!"

Pa. 75 = CBS 11094

1′. [ ] x [ ]
2′. [ ] ZU.IN IGI [ ]
3′. [ ] *um* IGI *Aḫ*$^{!}$-*i* x [ ]
4′. [ ] *Ir-ad-ì-lí*
5′. [ ] *ša* 3 GÍN KÙ.BABBAR
6′. [ ] *pá-ni-um i*
7′. [ ] x [ ]

Notes on Pa. 75 = CBS 11094

Mrs. Lewy described Pa. 75 as a "beautifully written black fragment of an envelope (impression of inner tablet visible on inside)—pitch black."

Line 2′ contains the latter part of a PN, [ ]-ZU.IN.

Line 3′ possibly has the PN *Aḫ*$^{!}$-*ilī*, although it looks like  followed by *i-a*[ ]. Mrs. Lewy suggested *Ah*$^{!}$-*ì-lí*, which is only remotely possible. The only PNs, besides *Aḫ-mar-ši* (see note on Pa. 7:20), known to me beginning in *Aḫ* are *Aḫ-Ša-lim*, *Aḫ*$^{?}$-*ší-ta* (ICK 2, 105 + 108:2), *Aḫ-Ištar* (ATHE 8:5; 36:22), and *A-aḫ-A-šùr* (CCT 1,

41b:3). The PN *A-aḫ*-DINGIR occurs in BIN 6, 41:2, 4; CCT 2, 7:28; CCT 3, 40b:2; and TC 1, 52:1.

Line 4′— The PN may be read *Ša*!*-at-ì-lí* although the *ša* is suspect. Although I cannot find Irad-ilī elsewhere, it parallels *Ir-ad-ku-bi₄-im* in MAH 10824:1, 3 (Garelli RA 59 [1965] 35–37) and *Ir-ad-ku-be* in TC 1, 43:19.

Pa. 76 = CBS 4045

1′. *ša* 1 GÍN [ ]
2′. *ṣí-pá-r*[*a*]
3′. *ša* 1 GÍN x [ ]
4′. *ṣa-áp-ru* x [ ]
5′. *ša* 22 1/2 [ ]
6′. DU-UG [ ]

Notes on Pa. 76 = CBS 4045

Line 2′ may be restored as *ṣí-pá-r*[*a-tum*, or *tim*]. See the note on Pa. 3:24.

I have no suggestion for line 4′, ZA.ÁB-*ru*?[ ]. One thinks immediately of associating this term with *ṣiparātum* (see line 2′ above and Pa. 3:24) and taking this form from *ṣapārum*, "to be pointed."

We probably have to restore either the PN *Du-ug*-[*la-nim*] in line 6′ (occurring in BIN 4, 173:28 [= EL 235]), or *Du-uq-li* appearing in Gelb 55:30.

Pa. 77 = CBS 4066

Edge 1′. [ ] *li-il₅-qí*
Rev. 2′. [*t*]*í*? *ša A-ki-dí-e*
3′. [ ]*lim*ki *ša-a-ma*
4′. [ ]⌈*šé*-⌉*ú-ni* [ ]
5′. [ ] *ša* / *a-ma* [ ]
6′. [ ] *ša* GA [ ]

Notes on Pa. 77 = CBS 4066

Mrs. Lewy remarked about Pa. 77 that it is the "upper right hand corner of reverse; beautiful script."

We may perhaps restore [TÚG-*t*]*í* or the like before *ša A-ki-dí-e* in line 2′.

Line 3′— We suggest [*ina* or *ana*] *a*$^{!}$-*lim*^{ki} with half of the *a* still visible on the text according to collation.

Pa. 78 = CBS 4040

	1′.	[	] ⸢*i*⸣ x [ ]
	2′.	[	] *bi*$_4$-*tí-kà*
	3′.	[	] *i-na ba-ri-šu-nu*
	4′.	[	] x *nu-ša-am*
	5′.	[	] ZI-*ru*
	6′.	[	] *me-tim*
Edge	7′.	[	] x
Rev.	8′.	[	]
	9′.	[	] *na*
	10′.	[	*i*]*m ša A-šùr*
	11′.	[	] *nam*
	12′.	[	*um*-]*ma a-ta-ma*
	13′.	[	] *ma*

Notes on Pa. 78 = CBS 4040

Pa. 78 is the lower right hand corner of a letter written in beautiful script.

Only a few words remain: *bītika* in line 2′, *ina barišunu* (line 3′), perhaps *nu-ša-am* from *ša'āmum* in line 4′, the DN Aššur in line 10′, and *umma attama* in line 12′.

Pa. 79 = CBS 5678

1′.	[	] *ta-nu* [ ]
2′.	[	] 1/2 GÍN TA [ ]
3′.	[	] *ta-ad-nu* [ ]
4′.	[	] 5 x [ ]

Notes on Pa. 79 = CBS 5678

We may possibly restore [TÚG$^{?}$.*ku*-]*ta-nu*[ ] on line 1′.

Linc 4′— The sign following 5 may be GÍN or, more likely, TÚG.

Pa. 80 = CBS 5668

1′. [*t*]*im*
2′. [ ] *uš-tim*
3′. [ ] x *ni*
4′. [ ] *ri-*⌜*im*⌝
5′. [ ] *ar-tim*
6′. [ ] *áb*
7′. [ ] *A-šùr*
8′. [ ] x

Notes on Pa. 80 = CBS 5668

Line 3′ may retain the traces of *tim* instead of *ni*.
Line 6′— The remains may be the back end of *tim* rather than *áb*.
The traces of line 8′ may perhaps be those of *tim*.

Pa. 81 = CBS 4085

1′. [ ] KÙ.BABBAR-*pí tù-kà-al* [ ]
2′. [ ] *sà-aḫ-ra-tí* 2 1/2 MA.[NA]
3′. [ ] *ú* 1/2 MA.NA 8 1/2 [GÍN?]
4′. [ ] *ṣa-ba-at-ma* x [ ]

Translation of Pa. 81 = CBS 4085

1′. [ ] You hold my silver [ ]
2′. [ ] You are stopping. 2 1/2 manas [ ]
3′. [ ] and 1/2 of a mana (and) 8 1/2 [shekels(?)]
4′. [ ] seize and x [ ]

Notes on Pa. 81 = CBS 4085

Pa. 81 is a fragment from the middle of a tablet.
Line 2′— We are taking the form *sà-aḫ-ra-tí* as a G stative from

saḫārum, "to turn (toward), seek, stop." See the notes on Pa. 11:13; 17:9; and 21:9 above.

Line 4′— The traces may indicate ŠU.NIGÍN or *ra*.

Pa. 82 = CBS 4084

1′. [ ] *nu* [ ]
2′. [ ] *šu* [ ]
3′. [ ] *šu a na* [ ]
4′. [ ] *i-a-tí li-dí-*[*na-*]*ku-ma*
5′. [G]A? *i-du-nu-ni*
6′. [ ]*a*!*-dí-šu-um*
7′. [ ] x *a ub-la-kum*
8′. [ ] x [ ]

Notes on Pa. 82 = CBS 4084

The fragment Pa. 82 is from the middle right side of a tablet.

Line 3′ may be interpreted as [ ]-*šu a-na* or as the PN *Šu-A-na* which possibly appears in BIN 6, 79:30. See Hirsch UAR 27f. for the native deity, Anna. The parallel PN Šāt-Anna is clearly attested as shown by Hirsch.

We read line 4′ [ ]*i-a-tí li-dí-na*!*-ku-ma* by picking up the *ku-ma* from the end of line 5′.

The first preserved sign on line 7′ is *ta*, *bi*, or *kà*. If *ta* is assumed, we may have the well known PN [*Bu-zu-t*]*a-a*.

ADDENDUM
SIZE AND DESCRIPTION OF THE PENNSYLVANIA OLD ASSYRIAN TEXTS

Pa. No.	Museum No.	Size*	Color	Line Drawing
1A	L 29–553 Tablet	**	reddish beige	HUCA 39 3
1B	L 29–553 Case	**	reddish beige	4
2	L 29–555	63×56×19	reddish tan	5
3	L 29–556	45×45×26	light reddish tan	7
4	L 29–557	92×62×21	light tannish brown	8
5	L 29–558	70×57×21	light reddish tan	11
6	L 29–559	68×48×19	light tannish brown	12
7	L 29–560	81×59×22	light tan	14
8	L 29–561	83×60×19	light reddish brown	15
9	L 29–562	60×55×21	light tan	17
10	L 29–563	62×48×21	light tan	19
11	L 29–564	51×46×19	light reddish tan	20
12	L 29–566	64×56×21	light reddish tan	21
13	L 29–567	69×58×19	light reddish tan	22
14	L 29–568	73×48×22	light reddish tan	24
15	L 29–569	69×55×22	light reddish cream	25
16	L 29–571	58×44×20	tan	27
17	L 29–572	48×44×16	obverse, light brown reverse, reddish brown	29
18A	L 29–573 Tablet	56×45×17	light tan	30
18B	L 29–573 Case	62×50×24	mostly cream (small areas of red)	31
19	L 29–574	59×48×17	light tan	32
20	L 29–575	55×46×17	reddish brown	HUCA 40/41 46
21	L 29–577	40×46×14	light brown	47
22	L 29–579	52×44×16	light brown	48

* All sizes are given in millimeters.

** Both Tablet and Case of Pa. 1 are on display and could not be measured.

Pa. No.	Museum No.	Size*	Color	Line Drawing
23A	L 29–580 Tablet	43×46×15	reddish brown	50
23B	L 29–580 Case = L 29–630 + L 29–585	58×48×27	reddish brown	51
24	L 29–581	47×45×17	tan	51
25	L 29–583	46×50×16	reddish tan	52
26	L 29–584	46×48×16	light brown	53
27	L 29–586	44×42×15	light reddish tan	55
28	L 29–587	52×53×17	brown	56
29	L 29–588	35×38×14	reddish brown	57
30	L 29–589	50×45×19	tan	58
31	L 29–590	42×43×15	light red	59
32	L 29–591	35×39×14	tan	60
33	L 29–592	43×39×12	light red	61
34	L 29–593	32×45×20	red	62
35	L 29–595	39×48×15	reddish brown	63
36	L 29–596	38×41×16	red	63
37	L 29–600	35×36×17	light red	64
38	L 29–601	41×43×15	creamy tan	65
39	L 29–602	33×39×17	tan	66
40A	L 29–603 Tablet	36×41×13	brown	66
40B	L 29–603 Case	48×46×20	brown	67
41	L 29–604	43×45×14	brown	68
42	L 29–606	44×48×18	brown	69
43	L 29–607	23×28×12	tan	70
44	L 29–610	34×47×16	dark tan	70
45	L 29–611	32×38×13	tan	71
46	L 29–612	60×38×18	dark beige (very weathered)	71
47	L 29–613	47×32×17	obverse, cream over red reverse, red	72
48	L 29–618	27×28×6	dark beige	73
49	L 29–619	49×31×13	tan	73
50	L 29–620	37×39×15	tan	73
51	L 29–622	35×37×16	tan	74

Pa. No.	Museum No.	Size*	Color	Line Drawing
52	L 29–623	28×37×13	reddish tan	75
53	L 29–624	24×31×14	light reddish tan	76
54	L 29–625	24×34×10	light brown	76
55	L 29–628	50×43×17	dark beige	76
56	L 29–629	19×45×15	dark beige	77
57	L 29–631	24×34×11	obverse, red	77
			reverse, cream over red	
58	UM 41–41–2	53×47×14	brown	78
59	CBS 4057	50×43×20	white	79
60	CBS 4072	29×30×16	dark tan	80
61	CBS 5675	30×31×13	beige	80
62	CBS 4074	20×31×16	obverse, dark gray	80
			reverse, gray	
63	CBS 4054	39×40×16	light beige	81
64	CBS 11092	41×27×14	beige	82
65	CBS 11095	31×17×10	light red	82
66	CBS 11091	15×15×6	reddish tan	82
67	CBS 11093	22×21×8	gray	82
68	CBS 5669	35×38×14	red	83
69	CBS 5672	32×39×10	reddish brown	83
70	CBS 5677	29×34×11	light red	83
71	CBS 5674	34×23×17	light reddish tan	83
72	CBS 5679	24×22×12	obverse, reddish brown	83
			reverse, red	
73	CBS 5670	45×26×13	red	84
74	CBS 4073	38×40×6	reddish tan	84
75	CBS 11094	35×35×7	dark gray	84
76	CBS 4045	29×28×14	red	84
77	CBS 4066	28×33×10	reddish brown	84
78	CBS 4040	32×21×17	dark beige	85
79	CBS 5678	23×28×12	cream	85
80	CBS 5668	64×33×16	tan over red	85
81	CBS 4085	18×29×10	red	85
82	CBS 4084	35×28×8	light red	85

INDICES

[br. = brother of; f. = father of; hus. = husband of; ḫ. = *ḫamuštum*-period (of); ib. = *ibidem*; k. = *kunukkum* (seal of); l. = *līmum*-eponym of; s. = son of; ṭup. = *ṭupšarrum* (scribe); w. = witness; ♀ = a female]

I. Personal Names

A-aḫ-Ištar 5:2
f. *A-šùr-na-ṣí-ir* 1:A 28, B 2
A-al-ṭāb (DU$_{10}$) 8:6 (*I-dí-A-šùr*, *kaṣṣār* of *A.*)
A-ba-tim
f. *Ku-ki-ni-im* 23:A 3, B 4′!
A-bi-a-a
f. *Ú-zu-a* 32:2
A-bi$_4$-li-a
f. *Ú-zu-a* 51:10
A-bu-Ša-lim, *Áb-Ša-lim*[1] 31:2[1], 12[1]; 37:8[1]
f. *A-šùr-ta-ak-lá-ku* 8:12
Adad-ellāt (^{d}IM-ILLAT) 23:A 19 w.
Adad-rabi (^{d}IM-GAL) 4:31
Adad-rē'um (^{d}IM-SIPA) 26:2, 4, 9, 18
Adad(^{d}IM)-*ṣú-lu-li* 2:27 w.
A-du 22:5
A-gu$_5$-tum, *A-gu$_5$-tim*[1] 4:7 l., 23 l.
l. *ša qāti A.* 4:40[1], 53[1]
A-ḫa-tim ♀ 29:1
Aḫ-i-[li?] 75:3′?
Aḫ-mar-ší 7:20 l.
Aḫ-Ša-lim 58:2
A-ḫu-qar, *A-ḫu-wa-qar*[1] 4:28 ḫ.; 21:1[1]; 23:A 4, B 5′; 57:5[1]
A-lá-ḫi-im, *A-la-ḫi-im*[1], *A-lá-ḫu-um*[2] 5:2[1]; 12:4; 13:5 (s. *A.*); 17:1[2]; 50:6, 10; 51:2; 58:2
s. *A.* 13:5
s. *Šál-ma-A-šur* 4:26
A-lá-ri-a 40:A 19 w., B 3 k.

A-šùr-mu-ta-bi$_4$-il$_5$
s. *Pu-šu-ki-in* 4:14
A-šùr-na-da, *A-šur-na-da*[1] 2:2, 7, 14; 3:1[1]; 6:1, 12; 8:1, 18; 10:2; 12:5; 13:2[1]; 14:2; 17:2; 24:1, 4; 30:1, 16; 39:2[1]; 50:2[1], 14[1]; 60:1″[?]
s. *Púzur-A-na* 23:A 16[1] 1.
h. *ša qāti Amurrum*(dMAR.TU)*-ba-ni* and *A*. 23:A 7[1], B 8′[1]
A-šùr-na-ṣí-ir
s. *A-aḫ-Ištar* 1:A 27 (*dajjānum*), B 2 k.
A-šur-rabi(GAL), *A-šùr-rabi*(GAL)[1] 37:10[1]; 43:1; 58:2[1], 39[?]; 65:2″ ([*A-*]*šur-rabi*(GAL))
s. *Lá-qí-pì-im* 4:43
uncle of *Ṭāb*(DU$_{10}$)*-A-šùr* and *Lá-qí-pì-im* 25:2[1], 4[1]
A-šur-ṣú-lu-li 51:3
A-šùr-ša-du-ni
f. *Ú-ṣur-ša-A-šùr* 37:4
A-šur-šamšī(UTU-*ši*), *A-šùr-šamšī*(dUTU-*ši*)[1] 44:5[1]
me-er-e A. 19:24
A-šùr-ta-ak-lá-ku, *A-šur-ta-ak-lá-ku*[1], *A-šur-ták-lá-ku*[2], *A-šur-ta-ak-la-ku*[3], *A-šùr-ták-lá-ku*[4] 5:3, 19; 6:2[1], 9, 14[1], 17[1]; 27:3[2]; 30:3[3] (<*ku*>); 38:6[4] (É *A*.); 39:13[1]
s. *A-bu-Ša-lim* 8:11
A-šur-ṭāb(DU$_{10}$) 22:2
A-šùr-[ ], *A-šur-*[ ][1] 68:5′; 70:1′[1]
Ba-ba-li, *Ba-bi-lim*[1]
f. *A-šùr-li-bi-i* 1:A 28, B 3[1]
Ba-lá-ṭá-a 5:20
Ba-ru-ki-in
hus. *Nu-ùḫ-ší-tim* 40:A 3, B 4 k.
Be-lúm-ba-ni 8:9
Bi-tí-tí, *Bi$_4$-tí-tí*[1] 58:1, 27[1], 33[1]
Bu-ra-a 58:26 (É *B*.)
Bu-za-zu 4:37
Bu-zi-a
f. *Ṭāb*(DU$_{10}$)*-ṣí-lá-A-šùr* 1:A 1, B 4
Bu-zu 41:2
Bu-zu-li-a 36:18 w.
Bu-zu-ta-a 34:4″; 73:3′[?] ([*Bu-*]*zu-ta-a*[ ])
Da-da-a 45:8 w.
Da-na-a 9:1, 3, 24
Dan-A-šur, *Dan-A-šùr*[1] 7:17; 19:11[1], 18[1] (*šēp D*.)

Za-lu-li 44:3
Zi-ra-bi 40:A 17 w., B 1 k.
ZU-*i-dá-dá* 36:6
Zu-pá
  ḫ. *Šu-Ku-bi*$_4$*-im* and *Z.* 12:9
Zu-ri-i 58:5
[-*A*-]*šùr* [ ] 34:5′
[-*A-šù*]*r* 60:2″; 80:7′
  s. *Púzur-A-šùr* 47:17
[-]*ri*$^{!}$*-iš* 55:1
[-]*Su'en*(ZU.IN) 49:4; 75:2′
[-]*Ša-lim* 61:2″$^{?}$
[-]*Šamaš*(^{d}UTU) 44:7

II. Līmum-*Eponyms*

A-gu$_5$*-tum* 4:7, 23
  l. *ša qāti A-gu*$_5$*-tim* 4:40, 53
Aḫ-mar-ší 7:20
A-šur-na-da
  s. *Púzur-A-na* 23:A 16
En-na-Su'en[ZU.IN) 4:46
  l. *ša qāti E.* 4:11
I-dí-a-bi$_4$*-im* 58:8
I-ku-pí-Ištar
  l. *ša qāti I.* 2:19
Ì-lí-a-lim 58:17
Ma-ṣí-ì-lí 4:17, 29, 35, 56

III. Ḫamuštum-*Eponyms*

A-ḫu-qar 4:28
Amurrum(^{d}MAR.TU)*-ba-ni*
  ḫ. *ša qāti A.* and *A-šur-na-da* 23:A 6, B 7′
A-šur-iš-ta-ki-il$_5$ 4:55
A-šur-na-da
  ḫ. *ša qāti Amurrum*(^{d}MAR.TU)*-ba-ni* and *A.* 23:A 7, B 8′
E-lá-lí

ḫ. *Šu-*^{d}*En-líl* and *E.* 36:9
En-nam-A-šur 4:33
s. *Šál-me-ḫi-im* 4:16
En-na-nim
s. *Šu-Ḫu-bu-ur* 4:4
I-dí-a-bi$_4$*-im* 4:51
I-ku-pì-a
s. *Šu-A-nim* 4:45
Kur-ub-Ištar 4:10
Lu-zi-na 4:38
Púzur-Ištar 4:22!
Šu-^{d}*En-líl*
ḫ. *Š.* and *E-lá-lí* 36:8
Šu-Ku-bi$_4$*-im*
ḫ. *Š.* and *Zu-pá* 12:9
Zu-pá
ḫ. *Šu-Ku-bi*$_4$*-im* and *Z.* 12:9

IV. Rabi(GAL) Šāqē *Official*

Na-ki-li-e-ed 40:A 6

V. Scribe (DUB.SAR)

Ḫa-nu-nu 52:16 w.

VI. Judges (Dajjānum)

A-šùr-li-bi-i
s. *Ba-ba-li* 1:A 28, B 3 k. (s. *Ba-bi-lim*)
A-šùr-na-ṣí-ir
s. *A-aḫ-Ištar* 1:A 27, B 2 k.
E-na-A-šùr
s. *Puzúr-A-na* 1:A 26, B 1 k.

VII. *Divine Names*

A-šùr, *A-šur*^{1} 1:A 7 (*ší-ga-ri-im ša A.*), B 8 (ib.); 7:37; 8:46; 10:15; 18:A 29^{1}; 33:14^{1}; 78:10′$^{?}$

Ilabrat(NIN.ŠUBUR) 7:38

Ilum(DINGIR), *Ilū*(DINGIR$^{hi.a}$)^{1}, *i-li-a*^{2}, *il_5-kà*^{3} 6:24^{1}, 26, 28, 32^{1}; 9:17 (*ba-áb* DINGIR), 32 (ib.); 10:7 (DINGIR *libbatika malli*); 17:29 (DINGIR *lu i-dí*); 18:A 30^{2}; 33:14^{3}

^{d}*Ištar* 10:18

Ni-ba-as 47:13 ([*ša*] *Ni-ba-a*[*s*])

VIII. *Geographical Names*

A-ki-dí-e 77:2′ ([TÚG-*t*]*í ša A.*)

A-lim^{ki}, *A-lim*^{1} 1:A 5 (*nīš a.*), B 6 (ib.); 2:12; 16:7, 34 (*awāt a.*), 36, 37; 17:31^{1}; 20:33; 28:12; 32:12; 35:1′ ([*a*-]*lim*^{ki}); 77:3′ (ib.)

(TÚG-)*Bu-ra-um* (nisbe?) 65:5″

Bu-ur-<*uš-*>*ḫa-tim* 16:5

Dur_4-ḫu-mì-id, *Du-ur-ḫu-mì-id*^{1} 2:21; 8:36^{1}; 28:16^{1}

Eq-lu-um, *Eq-lim*^{1}, *Eq-lam*^{2} 16:15, 35^{1}, 36^{1}; 41:5^{2}

Ḫa-bu-ra-ta-i-um (nisbe) 36:2

Ḫa-ḫi-im 17:6

Ḫa-tim 7:8

Ḫu-ra-ma 8:40; 19:29

Kà-ni-iš, *Kà-ni-ìš*^{1} 2:21; 8:49$^{!!}$; 17:13^{1}, 17 (*kārim K.*); 29:20^{1} (*ma-ḫi-ir K.*); 32:14; 62:2′ (*Kà-ni-i*[*š*])

Kà-ni-ší-ú (nisbe) 21:19

Kà-nu-e 19:33

Ku-na-na-ma-at 2:22

Ni-na-ša-a 20:22

Ša-lá-tù-wa-ar 29:5

Ta-wi-ni-a 9:11 (*kāram T.)*

Té-ga-ra-ma 27:8, 9

Tí-mì-il_5-ki-a 8:50; 17:27 (<*a*>)

Tí-iš-mu-ur-na 16:18

Wa-aḫ-šu-ša-na 21:13; 27:17

IX. Month Names

Áb Ša-ra-ni 4:52
A-lá-na-tim 4:46
*Be-el-tí-ekallim(*É.GAL*-lim*) 4:39
Ḫu-bu-ur 47:20 ([*Ḫ*]*u-bu-ur*)
Kán-mar-ta 4:17, 22, 35
Ku-zal-li 4:6
Ma-ḫu-ur-ilī(DINGIR) 2:18
Na-ar-ma-ak-A-šur 6:4
Qá-ra-a-tim 4:28
Ṣí-ip-im 23:A 15, B 13′
Ša Sà-ra-tim 4:10
Tí-i-na-tim 4:56

GLOSSARY

abākum 33:8, 20
abnum (*ša abnišu*) 8:5
abullum, see *bāb a.*
adāmum 14:18; 16:22; 30:29
adārum 58:23
adi išrīšu (= *ešrīšu*) 58:34
adīni 33:16
aḫa[?] 41:15
aḫamma 20:30; 58:10; 68:4′[?]
aḫātum 42:15
aḫāzum 41:12
ajjūm 24:15 (*a-i-tim*)
alākum 2:12; 5:33; 6:16; 7:8, 22; 8:14, 21, 36; 10:5, 24; 11:18; 16:6, 8, 15; 17:28; 19:16, 20; 20:22, 23; 22:25; 25:8, 18; 27:8, 13, 15, 16; 28:19; 29:13, 27; 35:5′; 43:11, 13; 50:9, 21; 52:10; 53:4; 61:4″
ālikum 28:7; 33:6
amārum 8:44; 30:27; 42:18
amma 18:A 17
amtum 31:7; 41:16
amūtum 63:3′, 6″[??]
ana bari 1:A 9, 18, B 10, 15
ana libbi 7:32
ana mala, see also *mala* and *ina mala*, 28:11; 30:20
ana qabli 18:B 10
ana ṣēr 2:4; 5:24; 8:19; 28:18, 31; 50:13; 58:31[!]
ana šūmi 6:18, 22; 10:6, 22; 14:3; 18:A 33; 29:23; 41:6
anāḫum 6:35
anni 5:23[!]; 18:A 8
anni'ūtum 1:A 29; 24:6
annītum lā annītum 29:26
anni'um 2:11; 5:34; 9:31; 12:19
annukum (AN.NA) 3:3, 15; 5:4, 10, 13, 18, 23; 6:15, 18, 19, 21, 36; 7:5, 23; 13:21, 25; 15:8, 37; 19:4, 13; 20:24; 22:3, 6, 10, 11, 13, 18, 22, 23; 30:8, 11[!!]; 32:5; 33:12

annukum qātum 15:8, 32
apālum 11:12; 16:21 (perhaps *tabālum*)
apputtum 6:9, 17, 24, 27; 14:9; 17:20, 20
aršātum 38:2, 18
aršatum (GIG) 47:7
assurri!! 73:2′
ašar 3:7; 5:20, 21; 6:38; 7:35, 39; 25:20; 31:12; 41:12; 59:7′?
ašārum 3:18
aššatum (DAM) 38:2; 45:4
aššatum 40:A 4, B 6
atā'um 6:30?
awātum 6:24; 9:18, 23; 14:32; 16:34; 18:A 33, B 3; 20:7, 32; 29:7, 12; 33:21; 52:2, 6
awīlum 1:A 29; 8:51, 52?; 9:10; 14:13; 18:A 10; 29:9; 41:8; 73:7′?
bāb abullim 3:5
bāb ḫarrānim, see *ḫarrānum*, 11:14f.
bāb ilim 9:17, 32
bābtum 17:30; 20:26, 28, 29; 21:14; 25:15
balāṭum 8:45; 42:5
balum 1:A 25, B 22; 8:38
barā'um (BRI) 6:10, 18
bašallum 8:5
bašā'um 14:12; 17:32; 19:31; 20:31; 22:24; 26:6, 7, 16; 28:35; 32:10; 37:13; 58:26
batāqum 2:17; 13:24; 29:19
be'ālum 5:28 (perhaps *ni'ālum*); 8:37; 16:10; 26:15
bēltum 29:4
bēlum 54:3
berdum, see *wardum*, 21:18
be'ulātum 8:41; 24:11; 32:16
bi'ādum 25:18
bītum (É) 6:22; 14:32, 36; 16:20; 31:9, 14; 38:5; 54:3; 58:26, 36; 73:6′; 78:2′
bu'ārum, see *ba'ārum*
bulṭum 18:A 33
(TÚG) *burā'um* 65:5″
dajjānum 1:A 29
dākum 11:23, 26
damqiš 19:34!
damqum (SIG_5) 22:4; 28:21, 26, 27; 36:2; 47:1

damum? 49:3
danānum 14:40; 29:7
dannat ilē(DINGIR$^{hi.a}$) 6:31f.
dannum 18:A 12
daš'um 6:11; 8:26
dātum 15:21
di'ānum 9:13
dudittum 31:4; 63:4′, 5′
du-ra-áš-ki? 43:14
ē 6:30, 31; 18:A 13?
ebrum, see *ibrum*
ēdum, see *wēdum*
egārum 24:8
ekallum (É.GAL) 17:6; 33:5
ela 8:41
elā'um 18:A 13?; 58:15
eliš, see *ištu . . . eliš*, 19:7
ellatum, see *illatum*
emārum 41:4, 5, 10
emārum (ANŠE$^{(hi.a)}$) 3:4; 15:15, 31, 34, 36; 19:19; 26:21, 29; 28:22, 28; 30:16, 21; 39:7; 74:3′!
emum 42:14
epāšum 1:A 16, B 16; 10:17; 18:B 9; 42:17
eqlum 8:51; 16:15; 41:5
erābum 3:7; 31:10; 32:15; 39:4
erāšum 16:11
eri'um (URUDU) 6:16; 8:21, 33, 37, 38, 42, 48, 49; 26:20, 23!, 27, 28; 30:18, 22, 28; 35:1′; 36:1, 16
eršum 25:8?
eṣārum 43:15
ēṣum 58:15
ešārum 28:6
ešertum 7:36
eširtum 15:24
ešrīšu, see *adi išrīšu*
etāqum 8:50; 27:12; 41:7
etellum 18:A 24, B 16
eṭārum 29:22
ezābum 20:26, 28; 25:23; 32:11; 37:9; 42:16; 43:6
gamālum 13:21; 29:16

gamārum 1:A 10, B 11, 15; 15:39; 52:4, 6
gamrum 3:20
gimillum 41:8
GIŠ.GA.ZUM (= *muštum*, which see)
ḫabālum 6:8; 10:15; 12:5; 13:13, 15; 16:23, 27, 30; 32:13; 38:7; 58:9, 12
ḫadā'um (ḪDU) 18:A 29; 68:8″
ḫalāqum 6:30; 18:A 27; 24:25
ḫamšīšu 6:25; 7:22
ḫamuštum 4:3, 9, 15, 21, 28, 33, 38, 44, 51, 55; 12:8, 10; 23:A 5, 8, B 6′, 9′; 36:7; 38:4
ḫarāmum 20:6
ḫarmum 13:17
ḫarrānum, see *bāb ḫarrānim*, 1:A 8, B 10; 5:23; 10:6; 28:4, 6; 31:18
ḫarrumum 2:20, 24
ḫasāsum 9:21, 23
ḫubullum 2:25; 11:8; 15:26
ḫuluqqā'um 35:7′, 8′??; 59:5′
ḫurāṣum (KÙ.GI, KÙ.KI) 8:4, 8, 14, 17; 10:14; 15:4; 17:3, 21; 48:3′; 63:1′
ḫurši'ānum 25:10; 26:19, 22, 24!
ḫuzīrum 24:8
ibrum 16:10
idā'um 3:12; 4:20; 8:46; 9:9, 19, 31 (perhaps from *nadā'um*); 16:35; 17:29
igrum 5:7; 43:7
ikribum 7:9, 28; 10:16, 19; 13:22
illatum (ILLAT) 19:12; 59:4′
ina bari 78:3′
ina ēṣim, see *ēṣum*
ina libbi 10:19; 25:11, 14; 26:6, 16; 32:6, 17; 57:3
ina maḫri 3:10f.
ina mala 8:40
ina migrātim 1:A 3, B 5
ina pānim 5:9, 30; 19:26f.; 39:8; 63:6″
ina ṣēr 4:1, 8, 13, 20!, 25, 31, 36, 43, 48, 54; 8:47; 14:37, 38; 17:12; 23:A 2, B 3′; 29:10, 17; 36:4; 40:A 2; 58:31?
ina šaḫātim 14:19f.; 27:10; 41:21
ina ūmēšu mal'uttim 36:12f.
inūmī 9:16, 29; 29:13

inūmīšuma 7:7
issurri$^{(?)}$ 73:2′
išārum, see *ešārum*
išātum 17:22
i-ší-ra-tim, see *eširtum*
iš-ra-at, see *ešertum*
išrīšu, see *adi išrīšu*
išrum 42:10
ištēn 18:A 19, B 12; 29:11
ištēniš (ŠU.NIGÍN) 6:21; 8:13; 15:6; 81:4′$^{?}$
ištu 2:18; 4:3, 9, 15, 21$^{!}$, 27, 33, 37, 44, 50, 55; 7:20; 8:25; 12:8; 13:27; 16:5, 26; 20:32; 23:A 5, B 6′; 36:7; 58:8, 16
ištu . . . eliš 18:A 25
išūm, see *laššu*, 4:3, 9, 15, 21, 27, 32, 37, 44, 50, 55; 20:19, 20; 23:A 5; 36:6; 40:A 8; 57:6; 58:37
itaṭlum 14:6, 9; 22:12
izāzzum 14:20; 17:15; 58:25, 36
kabāsum 15:10
kalā'um 16:13; 20:11; 24:11, 16
kamsum 15:14
kanākum 6:6, 8; 14:24; 22:30; 30:26; 37:16; 39:7; 58:31
karābum 10:23; 18:A 30
karpatum (DUG) 38:1, 4, 5, 8, 10, 11, 14
kārum 3:7; 4:8; 6:38; 9:11, 13; 17:17
kaspum ṣarrupum 2:1; 4:1, 8, 13, 19, 25$^{!}$, 30f., 42, 48, 54$^{!}$; 8:4, 7, 10, 22; 12:6f.; 13:29f.; 21:5; 22:28; 23:A 1f., B 2′f.; 30:4f.; 57:2
kaṣṣārum 8:6
kašādum 6:13; 7:12
ka''ulum 7:21; 8:19; 11:21; 16:16, 31, 34; 18:A 21, B 14; 24:15; 27:18; 41:17; 64:2′; 81:1′$^{!}$
ka''unum 1:A 22, B 21; 26:8
kēnum 5:25$^{!}$; 9:27; 17:16; 19:35; 26:10
kīam 22:13
kibtum (GIG), see *aršātum* (GIG)
kita'um 13:8
kubrum 36:10
kunukkum (KIŠIB) 1:B 1, 2, 3
kunukkum 3:3; 5:5; 8:5, 8, 11; 11:20, 25; 12:12; 15:8, 37; 20:31; 22:5, 14; 30:5; 31:4; 35:10′; 37:14; 45:2; 51:2; 58:22, 26
kusītum 7:8, 12, 23; 19:16

kutānum 3:4; 7:15, 24; 15:11, 13, 30; 22:4; 32:8; 39:10; 61:1′!, 5″!!; 79:1′!

lā libbi ilim 25:5

labāšum 63:2′?

lāma 33:18

lamānum 7:37, 42, 44; 16:12

lammunum, see *lummunum*

lamnum 29:9

lapātum 2:10; 8:32; 11:17; 39:12

laqā'um 2:14, 16; 3:17; 5:14, 16; 6:38; 7:7, 13, 27, 44; 11:7; 13:23, 26, 28; 14:16, 37, 39; 15:20; 16:24, 37; 17:13; 18:B 7; 20:30; 21:14, 18, 26; 26:21; 29:17; 31:16; 33:16; 41:14; 44:2, 3!, 5!, 7!; 50:20; 77:1′

laššu, see also *išūm*, 5:21; 20:23; 24:22; 25:19

lawā'um (LWI) 19:33

le'ā'um 13:20; 18:B 8; 33:23

libba (ŠÀ.BA) 8:15, 27; 15:7

libbātum 10:7

līmum 2:19; 4:7, 10, 17, 23, 29, 35, 39, 45, 53, 56; 7:20; 23:A 15, B 14′; 47:21!; 58:8, 17

liwītum 15:12

lubūšum 41:18

lummunum 26:27

luqūtum 5:31; 8:19; 14:6, 10, 31, 40; 18:A 23; 19:10; 33:19

mā 13:14

madādum 54:5

mādum 3:20; 5:14; 18:A 23; 35:1′; 55:Rvs. 10′

magārum 6:34

maḫārum 9:2, 12; 17:31

maḫīrum 29:20

mala, see also *ana mala* and *ina mala* 6:13; 8:33, 35, 38; 14:35; 17:30; 19:9, 19; 20:14; 46:2′?; 52:5; 58:37!

mala u šinīšu 22:16

malā'um 2:17; 8:49; 10:8; 18:B 15; 21:23; 30:20

māmītum 1:A 25, B 22; 14:26

mamman 20:23; 24:21; 35:3′?; 43:8

mānaḫtum 6:7

mannum 33:10; 43:5

maqātum 20:33; 24:9

marāṣum 18:A 32; 21:10; 22:26

marnu'ātum 38:15

maṣā'um (MṢI) 10:20; 14:33; 18:A 35; 29:20
mašā'um (MŠ') 2:26
mašā'um (MŠI) 6:32
maškum 8:28, 34
mašqaltum 6:3
maṭā'um 3:22 (perhaps from *patā'um*); 5:15; 15:25; 45:7
maṭû (LÁ) 44:2, 6; 48:2′
mazītum 38:9
meḫrātum 21:12
mērum 4:54; 14:19, 30; 18:A 5; 19:23; 23:A 4, B 1′, 5′; 53:3
mētum 8:52$^{!}$
migrātum, see *ina migrātim*
mimma annim 7:19; 15:27, 37; 19:25
-min, *-men*, see also *šummamin*, 16:32, 33
mīnum 13:12; 16:22; 20:17; 70:4″$^{?}$
mišlum 12:14; 14:11, 23; 58:20, 23, 24, 29
miššum 8:48; 13:3; 42:3
mu'ātum 12:20; 15:37; 25:7, 7; 35:6′; 71:6′$^{?}$
mu'ā'um 8:32
munūtum 3:9, 12
mūṣi'um 54:4
mušṭum (GIŠ.GA.ZUM) 64:4′$^{?}$
muttatum 3:16; 72:7′$^{???}$
muṭā'ū 72:7′$^{???}$
na'ādum 17:25; 18:A 4, B 4$^{!}$; 33:9, 23
nadānum, see *šīmam nadānum*, 1:A 24, B 13, 21; 2:3, 6, 8; 3:14; 5:8, 12, 12, 19; 6:20, 21, 26; 7:25, 32, 35, 39, 43; 8:17, 18, 30, 40, 43, 50; 9:7, 10, 18, 30; 10:11, 26; 11:23, 26; 12:13; 13:30; 14:7, 10, 31; 15:27; 16:11; 18:A 24; 19:8, 9, 37; 21:8, 12, 19, 23, 26; 22:7, 9, 12, 23, 24, 27; 26:15, 18, 21$^{!}$, 30; 28:34; 30:9, 29; 31:21; 35:10′; 37:19; 38:3, 5, 11, 13, 16; 41:4, 13; 47:12; 50:17; 53:6; 58:22, 33, 38; 64:2″$^{!}$; 82:4′, 6′
nadā'um 1:A 15; 5:17, 26; 6:17; 7:33; 8:38; 9:19 (perhaps from *idā'um*); 10:22; 32:7; 33:17
naḫādum, see *na'ādum*
naḫlaptum 63:7′$^{!}$
nakāmum 19:5
nakārum 26:7
nakāšum 6:28
napaštum 55:9′
naruqqum 10:10; 14:13; 38:1; 47:7; 53:1; 54:1; 63:1″

nasāḫum 26:13
naṣārum 6:25; 24:20, 23
našā'um 8:12; 9:22; 10:12; 14:14; 18:A 18, B 6, 11; 22:5; 30:7, 18; 31:6; 39:15; 61:2′
našpartum 8:31; 20:12, 34; 27:5; 52:1, 11
naṭālum 7:38; 33:15
ni'ālum 5:28
nibrārum 19:17
nikištum (*nikistum*$^{?}$) 6:28
nikkassum 5:16; 32:3; 50:5
nisḫatum 2:5
nīš ālim^{ki} 1:A 4, B 6
nu'ārum 38:12
panā'um 58:13
panītamma 20:35
pānī'um, see *ina pānim*, 2:25; 5:29; 8:20; 28:7; 33:7; 37:14; 75:6′$^{?}$
paqādum 3:6, 9; 19:35; 28:23, 30; 29:24; 51:4; 52:5; 62:4′
parakannum, see *pirikannum*
paṣi'um 7:9
pašārum 6:27
patā'um 3:22 (perhaps from *maṭā'um*); 14:34; 18:A 34, B 13; 22:17, 19; 29:25
pati'um, see *ūmū pati'uttum*
patrum (GÍR) 9:2
paṭārum 37:12; 45:5
pirikannum 8:28, 34, 42; 21:20, 22; 26:12; 29:18
pūm 6:26; 18:B 15
purūm 17:18
qa (SÌLA) 31:15
qādum 15:12
qanūm 19:33 (perhaps a GN)
qaqqarum 18:A 11
qaqqudum, see *rakāsum*
qēmum 54:2
qi'āpum 6:34, 37
qi'āšum 6:35; 14:15; 18:A 28
qibā'um 7:17; 20:27
qīptum 6:33; 22:29
qurbum, see *ūmū qurbuttum*
ra'āmum 18:A 6, 16, 22

rabā'um (RBI) 31:13
rabi(GAL) *šāqē* 40:A 7
radā'um 9:24; 13:16; 15:28, 38
ragmum 17:11
rakābum 16:17
rakāsum 12:24–26; 47:15f.
ramānum 10:3, 21; 18:A 31; 20:21; 33:17
rašā'um 31:19; 41:20, 22; 42:4, 7
rēšum 2:7
ri'āḫum (RIḪ) 38:19
ru'āqum 7:41; 17:26
sa'atum 15:19, 23
saḫartum 1:A 12, B 12
saḫārum 11:13; 17:9; 21:9; 30:28; 81:2′
salā'um (SLI) 17:27
sanāqum 26:25
sarādum 30:23
sardum 31:15
sāridum 5:7
si'āqum 28:3[?]
sikkum 16:31
subrum 24:5, 21, 24
ṣabātum 1:A 4, B 6; 13:7, 10, 12, 14; 14:27; 18:A 8, 14, 26; 24:19; 25:9, 13, 16; 26:2; 28:9; 35:8′; 81:4′
ṣābum 7:36
ṣaḫḫirum 8:42
ṣaḫir rabi 49:1[!!]
ṣallāmum 3:4; 15:16; 28:22, 28
ṣa-áp-ru[???] 76:4′
ṣarāpum 17:7
ṣibtam uṣṣab 4:6, 12, 18, 24, 30, 34, 41, 47, 53, 57; 21:25; 23:A 13f., B 12′f.; 29:14; 36:17; 40:A 15f., B 13[!]; 58:9, 18, 20, 24, 30; 70:4″[???]
ṣiparātum 3:24; 76:2′[??]
ṣubātum (TÚG[(ḫi.a)]) 3:8; 5:5, 11, 15, 17, 24; 6:36; 7:28, 29, 30; 19:4, 14; 20:19, 25; 22:11, 31; 28:20, 21, 21, 26, 27, 33; 30:9; 34:1′, 2′, 4′[!], 1″, 2″, 3″, 4″, 5″; 49:7[?]; 77:2′[?]
ṣuḫartum 7:29; 31:5
ṣuḫārum 15:22; 20:9, 13; 31:11, 21
ṣuḫrum 41:19
ša abnišu, see *abnum*

ša qātim 15:12, 32; 28:21, 27
ša'āmum 19:19; 21:21, 22, 24; 28:13; 35:9′; 77:3′; 78:4′?
šabārum 8:47; 24:10
šabā'um 5:7; 11:19; 12:15; 20:25?; 58:21
šabburum 36:3
šadādum 22:18
šaddū'atum 2:5
šaḫātum, see *ina šaḫātim izāzzum*
šaḫātim 16:29, 32
šāḫirum 42:11
šakākum? 16:14; 18:B 9?
šakānum 3:16; 8:52; 9:5, 26, 28; 14:29; 16:25; 17:18; 20:9; 37:15
šalāḫum 3:8
šalāmum 28:7; 43:16; 62:3′
šalāš 9:20
šalmum, see *rakāsum*
šamā'um 7:33; 14:22; 18:A 19, 34, B 13; 20:13; 25:17; 27:6; 33:22; 55:6′?
šamnum 42:12
šamšum (dUTU) 20:12; 24:17
šamšum 25:16; 27:4, 13
šamšum, "sun emblem," 10:13
šani'um 6:37, 38; 16:20; 50:4
šapārum 3:10, 19, 21; 5:9; 6:19, 22, 23; 7:26, 43; 8:40; 13:4; 16:3; 18:A 9; 19:22, 31; 20:3, 35; 22:21; 25:21; 28:11, 15, 25; 35:9′; 50:15; 58:35
šaptum (SÍGḫi.a) 41:17; 74:3′
šaptum 20:20
šarrum 33:18
šaršarānum 38:14, 17
šasā'um 32:4
šattišamma 7:35
šattum 2:2; 11:10
šazzuztum 11:4; 52:9
še'ā'um 12:17, 24, 27; 77:4′??
šēbultum 7:14
šēpum 5:13, 32; 7:15; 15:38; 19:10, 18; 24:9; 30:10
še'um (ŠE) 47:8, 9; 53:2
ši'amātum 8:39; 14:21
ši'ātum 8:35

šību̅m 13:16; 14:29, 39; 20:5; 61:5′?
šībūtum 9:5, 7, 25, 28
ší-ga-ri-im 1:A 6, B 8
šīmam nadānum 14:22f.
šīmtum 11:12; 19:28; 71:10′?
šīmum 17:32; 19:18; 21:17, 24; 26:12, 20, 26, 28, 29; 28:13; 29:18; 30:8; 33:12; 39:6; 41:10, 14; 68:9″??
šinīšu 2:11; 17:23; 22:16; 68:10″??
šita 9:20
šeššīšu 6:25
šummamin 16:29
šuqlum 3:22; 7:6; 13:25
šūt 58:26
tabālum 8:34; 15:15, 31; 16:21
tabā'um 5:33; 10:4; 27:7
tadānum 8:33; 19:9; 79:3′??
takālum 33:11
tamalagum 37:5, 9, 11, 15; 63:3″??, 4″?
tamā'um 1:A 5, 5, 19, B 7, 7, 17
tamkārum (DAM.GÀR) 5:25, 26!; 41:1
tamkārum 30:19!; 35:7′; 41:6
tamkāruttum (DAM.GÀR-*ru-tum*) 25:15
tapalātum 38:10
tappā'um 9:14, 21
tappa'ūtum 1:A 16, B 16
tarbītum 31:20
tîrtum 7:21; 8:20, 35, 38; 19:15, 20; 22:25; 27:11, 14; 28:18; 29:25; 30:14, 21; 50:10, 20; 52:9; 61:3″
tu'ārum 6:29, 31; 17:8, 14, 19, 23; 20:8; 31:15; 38:8; 58:30
tù-ra-áš-ki (or [*ú-*]*tù-ra-e*!*-ki*) 43:14
ṭābum(DU_{10}) 26:28
ṭaḫā'um 28:24; 29:10
ṭarādum 6:10, 11; 8:51; 16:7; 20:15; 25:24; 28:5, 10, 32
ṭātum, see *dātum*
ṭi'ābum 31:17
ṭuppum 2:9, 20, 24; 5:33; 7:4; 8:16, 30; 9:6, 9, 15, 17, 29, 31; 11:15, 20, 22, 24; 12:2, 11, 19; 13:17; 14:21, 39; 16:3; 18:A 8, 17, 19, 20, 34, B 3, 4, 6, 12, 14; 19:28, 31, 33; 22:20; 25:17; 35:9′; 39:11; 43:4; 52:1, 13; 56:3″, 4″!; 58:21, 25, 31, 32, 40; 68:7″?
ṭupšarrum (DUB.SAR) 52:16

ukultum 15:18
ūmakal 58:35
ummi'ānum 6:3; 19:34
ummum 29:4
ūmū pati'uttum 19:8
ūmū qurbuttum 19:6
ūmū tamkārim 30:19
unūtum 15:17, 34; 33:4, 7; 63:2″
urram 14:26
urrum 16:26
[*ú*-]*tù-ra-e*[!]*-ki* (or *tù-ra-áš-ki*) 43:14
uṭṭutum (ŠE) 4:11; 44:2, 4, 6; 57:1
uṭṭutum 36:11
uznum 29:25
wabālum 3:23, 25; 5:6, 21, 22, 31; 6:15; 7:11, 19, 31; 8:6, 10, 26, 31; 10:20; 13:18; 14:4, 8, 11, 25, 28; 15:5; 17:32; 18:B 7; 19:27, 32, 35, 36; 21:15, 16, 21, 28; 28:12; 30:10, 13, 29; 33:13; 39:9; 41:15, 19; 42:13; 50:11; 58:39; 61:4′; 62:3″[!!]; 82:7′
wabartum 9:1
wadā'um, see *idā'um*
waklum 18:A 1, B 1
warā'um 24:19; 30:17
wardum 24:16
wardum (ÌR) 19:12
wardūtum 10:25
warkat 7:18
warki 5:34
wasmum 13:26
waṣā'um 3:5; 7:12; 9:3; 14:12; 24:7; 26:20, 23; 30:25; 37:10
waṣītum 15:35
wašābum 5:22; 8:49; 18:A 12; 20:15, 18; 24:5; 25:20; 27:11; 28:17; 33:19; 41:22
wašārum 8:49, 51; 14:8, 40; 29:6; 30:22; 43:9; 52:12
watārum (DIRIG) 2:15
wēdum 13:29
zakā'um 5:32; 6:23; 10:4; 19:14; 20:21; 22:17, 19; 29:12; 30:24
zakūtum 3:18
zarā'um 13:9